T0295855

Social Innovation in the Service of Social and Ecological Transformation

This book explores how the State can play a role as an enabler of citizens-led social innovations, to accelerate the shift to sustainable and socially just lifestyles.

To meet the twin challenges of environmental degradation and the rise of inequalities, societal transformation is urgent. Most theories of social change focus either on the role of the State, on the magic of the market, or on the power of technological innovation. This book explores instead how local communities, given the freedom to experiment, can design solutions that can have a transformative impact. Change cannot rely only on central ordering by government, nor on corporations suddenly acting as responsible citizens. Societal transformation, at the speed and scope required, also should be based on the reconstitution of social capital, and on new forms of democracy emerging from collective action at the local level. The State matters of course, for the provision of both public services and of social protection, and to discipline the market, but it should also act as an enabler of citizen-led experimentation, and it should set up an institutional apparatus to ensure that collective learning spreads across jurisdictions. Corporations themselves can ensure that society taps the full potential of citizens-led social innovations: they can put their know-how, their access to finance, and their control of logistical chains in the service of such innovations, rather than focusing on shaping consumers' tastes or even adapting to consumers' shifting expectations. With this aim in mind, this book provides empirical evidence of how social innovations, typically developed within "niches", initially at a relatively small scale, can have society-wide impacts. It also examines the nature of the activism deployed by social innovators, and the emergence of a "do-it-yourself" form of democracy.

This book will appeal to all those interested in driving societal change and social innovation to ensure a sustainable and socially just future for all.

Olivier De Schutter is the United Nations Special Rapporteur on Extreme Poverty and Human Rights. De Schutter previous served as Secretary General of the International Federation for Human Rights (FIDH) and the United Nations Special Rapporteur on the Right to Food, a mandate which he fulfilled between 2008 and 2014. He is also a Professor of Law at UCLouvain and at SciencesPo, France, and is a member of the Global Law School Faculty at New York University, USA. He is the co-editor of the *Routledge Handbook of Food as a Commons* (2018).

Tom Dedeurwaerdere is Professor of Philosophy of Science at the Université catholique de Louvain (UCL), Louvain-la-Neuve, Belgium. He is director of the research unit BIOGOV and co-founder of the Open partnership research on Ecological and Social Transition. He is the author of *Sustainability Science for Strong Sustainability* (2014).

Routledge Focus on Environment and Sustainability

For more information about this series, please visit: www.routledge.com/Routledge-Focus-on-Environment-and-Sustainability/book-series/RFES

Social Innovation in the Service of Social and Ecological Transformation
The Rise of the Enabling State

Olivier De Schutter and Tom Dedeurwaerdere

Routledge
Taylor & Francis Group
LONDON AND NEW YORK

from Routledge

First published 2022
by Routledge
2 Park Square, Milton Park, Abingdon, Oxon OX14 4RN

and by Routledge
605 Third Avenue, New York, NY 10158

Routledge is an imprint of the Taylor & Francis Group, an informa business

© 2022 Olivier De Schutter and Tom Dedeurwaerdere

The right of Olivier De Schutter and Tom Dedeurwaerdere to be
identified as authors of this work has been asserted in accordance
with sections 77 and 78 of the Copyright, Designs and Patents
Act 1988.

Trademark notice: Product or corporate names may be trademarks
or registered trademarks, and are used only for identification and
explanation without intent to infringe.

British Library Cataloguing-in-Publication Data
A catalogue record for this book is available from the British Library

Library of Congress Cataloging-in-Publication Data
Names: Schutter, Olivier de, author. | Dedeurwaerdere, Tom,
author.
Title: Social innovation in the service of social and
ecological transformation : the rise of the enabling state /
Olivier De Schutter, Tom Dedeurwaerdere.
Description: New York, NY : Routledge, 2022. |
Series: Routledge focus on environment & sustainability |
Includes bibliographical references and index.
Identifiers: LCCN 2021032769 (print) | LCCN 2021032770 (ebook)
Subjects: LCSH: Social change. | Social action. | Community
development. | Political participation.
Classification: LCC HM831 .S358 2022 (print) | LCC HM831
(ebook) | DDC 303.44—dc23
LC record available at https://lccn.loc.gov/2021032769
LC ebook record available at https://lccn.loc.gov/2021032770

ISBN: 978-1-032-12192-5 (hbk)
ISBN: 978-1-032-12198-7 (pbk)
ISBN: 978-1-003-22354-2 (ebk)

DOI: 10.4324/9781003223542

Typeset in Times New Roman
by codeMantra

Contents

1 The dusk of the consumer society and the role of social innovation

In the acceptance speech she delivered on 8 December 2009 when she was awarded the Nobel Prize in Economics, Elinor Ostrom suggested that "a core goal of public policy should be to facilitate the development of institutions that bring out the best in humans" (Ostrom, 2010). In this book, we explore what such a public policy could look like.

The growth model of advanced economies since the end of the Second World War has been based on increased consumer spending and the intensive use of non-renewable energy resources. This model is now in crisis, and the search for alternatives has started. Some believe only the strong hand of the State can bring about the transformation we need: we need to recapture the State, according to this view, or to "re-democratize" it, in order to impose the change from the top (Galbraith, 2008; Freeman, 2017). Others instead put their hopes in the power of critical consumers, whose choices are increasingly guided by sustainability-related concerns: provided we empower consumers, this version suggests, and the market actors shall have to adapt, leading our entire production model to be reformed.

We explore a different hypothesis. We suggest that local communities, given the freedom to experiment, can design solutions that can have a transformative impact. Change cannot rely only on central ordering by government, nor on corporations suddenly acting as responsible citizens. Societal transformation, at the speed and scope required, also should be based on the reconstitution of social capital, and on new forms of democracy emerging from collective action at the local level. The State matters, of course, both for the provision of public services and of social protection, and to discipline the market. But it should also act as an enabler of citizens-led experimentation, and it should set up an institutional apparatus to ensure that collective learning spreads across a jurisdiction. Corporations themselves can ensure that society taps the full potential of citizens-led social

DOI: 10.4324/9781003223542-1

innovations: they can put their know-how, their access to finance, and their control of logistical chains in the service of such innovations, rather than seeking to shape consumers' tastes or simply adapting to consumers' shifting expectations.

The new role we propose for the State – what we call the "Enabling State" – is not a substitute for the post-war Welfare State, with its characteristic mix of labour regulations and of redistributive social protection mechanisms. The Welfare State thus conceived remains essential to regulate market relationships and to compensate for the inequalities that have their source in market relationships – indeed, we explain in this book why inequalities are a major obstacle to the social and ecological transition. Rather, the Enabling State should complement the Welfare State, by addressing the organization of societal transition processes towards socially inclusive and environmentally sustainable well-being. The Enabling State seeks to support local experimentation and accelerate collective learning, both within countries and across countries. It collaborates with citizens' initiatives and initiatives from local public authorities and communities. The Enabling State encourages autonomy and reflexivity, i.e., the ability of individuals to challenge dominant social norms/received understandings about what "progress" and "success" mean, and indeed, how "happiness" or "well-being" are to be defined. It is not simply another way to regulate conduct: instead of prescribing conduct or "nudging" individuals in their choices, the Enabling State gives priority to equipping individuals to be autonomous and to experiment, both alone and with others.

Our proposals for the Enabling State are premised on the conviction that the kind of social transformation we require – large-scale, resulting in major and rapid shifts in production and consumption – requires all segments of society to contribute to change. Such transformation cannot depend only on the State apparatus, or on an improved functioning of the market ("green capitalism"), or on the social innovations within civil society. The view that any single one of these levers, considered in isolation, might suffice, fails on a number of counts.

First, such a view tends to idealize what any of these spheres can achieve, as if society could be changed by governmental decrees, by a sudden conversion of market actors to the requirements of sustainability under the pressure of critical consumers, or by the energy of citizens mobilizing for change by changing their immediate environment. We believe it is much more realistic to see each of these spheres as dependent on the others so that none of them alone shall be able to make a significant contribution to the transition required: it is only by these different spheres moving alongside one another and mutually supporting each other, that progress can be achieved.

Second, an understanding of the social transformation that sees any of these spheres as capable of provoking the shift required fails to see how, within each sphere, new ways of contributing to change may emerge, that support the transformations required in the other spheres. For instance, there are other ways for the central government to support change than by the adoption of top-down regulations and economic incentives that force private actors to absorb the full social costs of their activities (to "internalize negative externalities", in economists' jargon): governments could devolve power to local entities in order to favour a territorial approach to transition; they could influence the direction of innovation within private firms, and at the same time support the emergence of a more pluralistic economy; and they could create a framework enabling social innovations led by ordinary citizens. Similarly, it is difficult to conceive of citizens' initiatives that can have a lasting impact, while remaining more or less disconnected from market imperatives. While such initiatives can start, and even survive for a number of years, based solely on the voluntary contributions of participants and on the shared management of "commons", it is probably fair to say that they can only last and fulfil their transformative potential if they are also economically viable – if, in other terms, the rewards at least match the investment made (though neither the rewards nor the investments should be reduced to purely monetary terms). In other terms, we need to move beyond the opposition between a transition operating "from above" and a transition operating "from below", just like we need to move beyond the opposition between a transition that is "state-led" and one that is "market-led". We need to understand how the dynamics can be launched that allow all these shifts to support one another, rather than seeing any as a substitute for the other.

The time to do so is now. This is not only because the ecological transition is urgently needed if we want to avoid the worst and most unpredictable impacts of the heating of the planet and of biodiversity loss. It is also because of the political window that exists: the impatience with the dominant growth model is increasing, and there is a risk that certain segments of the population, especially within the younger generation, will turn more radical in their means of protest. If such radicalization leads to the emergence of new divisions within the social movement for change, making collective action more difficult to achieve because of tactical disagreements, the moment will be lost. Against this background, the major economic and social crisis triggered by the Covid-19 pandemic provides a once-in-a-generation chance for a recast of our development model: "Building Back Batter" is a slogan used by UN Secretary-General António Guterres to urge for a reset, but it also expresses a deep aspiration of large segments of society, which have now come to the realization that societal transformation at a large scale is not only conceivable but also realistic – indeed, more realistic perhaps than a return to business as usual.

This therefore is a time of opportunity. There is, indeed, a growing consensus about our predicament, and about the need to fundamentally rethink our model of growth. This model is unsustainable even from the purely macroeconomic point of view. The 2008–2009 financial crisis was the first significant warning signal. That crisis already shed light on the fragility of a model based on inflated levels of debt, both of households and of States (Streeck, 2014), and many observers noted that future shocks, once the financial markets shall rate the risks as too high, are likely. The more recent crisis triggered by the stillstand of the economy to slow down the Covid-19 pandemic not only results in an even less stable economic environment, but also demonstrates the feasibility of radical, society-wide change where there is both sufficient political will and population-wide support. Never have societal institutions seemed as far apart from the laws of nature.

The chief reason why we cannot continue along the current trajectory is that our model is destructive of the various capitals we rely on – the human capital of the workforce, the natural capital of the ecosystems, and the social capital of trust within societies. Our societies have been pursuing growth aggressively since the Second World War. Indeed, it is still largely on the basis of that measure of success that governments lose or win elections, and most people still see growth as progress. Indeed, economic growth (the increase of monetary wealth, as measured in GDP per capita) is still seen as indispensable to ensure that debts (whether public or private) are sustainable; it is considered vital to allow governments to collect taxes, in order to finance the public services it provides to the population; and it is still perceived by many as the only way both to address poverty and to create jobs. But economic growth increasingly resembles the golden cage already denounced by Weber in his classic analysis of the spirit of capitalism (Weber, 1905): although it presents itself as without alternative, it has trapped us into an unsustainable model of development and has proven unable to fulfil its promises in the long term. It now turns out that we have been exhausting ourselves in the pursuit of an illusory goal. Like sleepwalkers, we can continue to move towards the cliff. Or we can choose to wake up.

We explore how citizens-led social innovations can contribute to changing the course of societies, and how the State can help ensure that their potential is maximized. In Chapter 2, we review a number of myths that continue to pervade the discussion. In dispelling these myths, we hope to convince the reader that we cannot afford to ignore the transformative potential of social innovations: while other tools can serve such a transformation, more could and should be done to ensure that the imagination of communities is built upon and that we accelerate collective learning. Next, we explore in Chapter 3 how social innovations, typically developed within "niches", initially at a relatively small scale, can have society-wide impacts – in other terms, to use the language of the multi-level perspective on transitions, result in "regime change". By contrasting four scenarios of how niche innovations relate to the mainstream regime, we seek to identify the conditions under which social innovations can escape co-optation and instead play a genuinely subversive role, forcing the regime to recast itself. We find that two conditions in particular are decisive. First, a shared under-standing, across all the actors involved, of the sustainability challenges to be addressed and of how their individual strategies may contribute to addressing these challenges, may help ensure that the transforma-tive potential of social innovation is maximized. Second, whereas the incumbents of the mainstream regime may be tempted to choose how to incorporate the social innovation they have an interest in adopting, which is the very definition of co-optation, such instrumentalization of social innovation is much less likely to occur where the social innova-tors themselves participate in defining how such adoption shall occur.

In the remainder of the book, we move from theory to practice – from the idea of social innovations to its implementation. Chapter 4 examines the nature of the activism deployed by social innovators, which we see as very different from the kind of activism of earlier gen-erations. We document the current discontent with classic forms of collective action, through political parties or unions, and the emer-gence of a "do-it-yourself" form of democracy. In a nutshell: the pri-ority of activists today is to do things, not to call upon others to have things done. Expanding on a framework initially developed by Albert Hirschman on civic engagement, we identify the opportunities that emerge from this new form of engagement. Chapter 5 then discusses six concrete proposals that could support the emergence of citizens-led social innovations, ranging from the organisation of research to the support of the social and solidarity economy and from the promotion of sustainable finance to the shift in public action from the imposition of mandates to the encouragement of local experimentation.

We close, finally, by offering the broad outlines of a programme to reconceive the role of the state, as an enabler of social innovations. In Chapter 6, we emphasize in particular the role of indicators of progress that can provide workable alternatives to gross domestic product (GDP), to ensure that the transformation of society is steered in the right direction; as well as the need to include support to social innovations as a key component of the transition to sustainable societies, which we describe as the "18th Sustainable Development Goal". Chapter 7, finally, provides a more concrete picture of the "Enabling State" we call for. It describes the role of the State in addressing inequalities, in organizing geographical space, and in establishing spaces that can allow social innovations to flourish and that reward experimentation. Indeed, we see the reduction of inequalities, urban planning, and local experimentation as important "enablers", which the States may rely on in order to tap the potential of citizens-led social innovations to drive societal transformation.

The challenge, ultimately, is to rebuild the social capital required – a combination of trust and social norms providing the "cement" of society – to facilitate collective action and to maximize the potential role of social imagination in bringing about new lifestyles, allowing us to remain within planetary boundaries while at the same time ensuring well-being and, yes, happiness. The ecological transition should not be seen as imposing sacrifices, rationing, or dullness: it can be seen as an opportunity to rethink society in ways that will increase conviviality and solidarity, and that will reduce the pressure from competition and the drive for performance. This is a revolution from which all can gain, and social innovations have a key role to play in making it happen.

References

Freeman, D. (2017). De-Democratisation and rising inequality: The underlying cause of a worrying trend. Working Paper 12, Department of Anthropology and International Inequalities Institute, London School of Economics.

Galbraith, J. (2008). *The Predator State. How Conservatives Abandoned the Free Market and Why Liberals Should Too.* New York: Free Press.

Ostrom, E. (2010). Beyond markets and states: Polycentric governance of complex economic systems. *American Economic Review, 100*(3): 641–672.

Streeck, W. (2014). *Buying Time: The Delayed Crisis of Democratic Capitalism.* New York: Verso.

Weber, M. (1905). Die protestantische Ethik und der Geist der Kapitalismus. *Archiv für Sozialwissenschaft und Sozialpolitik, 20*(1): 1–54 & *21*(1): 1–110.

2   Obstructing myths

The contribution of citizens-led social innovations to the ecological and social transition shall only be recognized once we escape a number of myths that obstruct the understanding of how such a transition can succeed. Four myths in particular are persistent. Such myths provide a convenient pretext either to delay action on the social and ecological crises we face, or to minimize the potential of communities taking action to provide solutions – and, therefore, the need to support such action. They therefore perpetuate the idea that the dominant model of development, based on increased consumer spending and material growth, can be amended, and that the incumbent actors who dominate the mainstream regime are well placed to transform it. We suggest instead that this model of development has failed and should be more radically transformed; and that we can only achieve this by putting our hopes in the imaginative potential of citizens-led social innovations. But first, the myths must be deconstructed.

Myth #1 That technology alone (green, clean) shall suffice

Technology – cleaner, greener, more efficient – has a major role to play in allowing societies to win the race against time that has started against the degradation of the ecosystems and the loss of balance in essential global life-supporting processes. Indeed, the Ehrlich/Holdren equation, that long defined the parameters determining our ecological footprint (I), referred to technology (T), alongside population growth (P) and affluence (A), as a key factor to consider (Ehrlich and Holdren, 1971; Commoner, 1972). This influential equation ($I = P \times A \times T$) was thus premised on the idea that technological progress can compensate for the rising levels of resource use and pollution that accompany the rise of the mass consumption society. It still provides

DOI: 10.4324/9781003223542-2

the best summary of the idea of "green growth", according to which we can achieve a sustainable, low-carbon society by a combination of green investments as well as "the development and diffusion of clean technologies, for example, carbon capture and storage, renewable energy technologies, and application of green ICT for raising energy efficiency, and the development of an international market for environmental goods and services", to borrow a phrase from the 2009 OECD Ministerial Declaration on Green Growth. Technological advances, according to this view, would be able to cancel the impacts not only of demographic growth or of higher levels of consumption per capita but also of the two combined.

The belief that technological progress alone can achieve this extraordinary prowess strikes us as not only naive but also as potentially pernicious. Its first consequence is that it entertains the false idea that "green growth" is a viable option – in other terms, that it would be possible to continue to pursue the increase of GDP per capita while offsetting the ecological impacts through technological advances. This is a dangerous illusion. Economic growth mechanically leads to an increase in the ecological footprint, combining both resource depletion and the production of waste, including greenhouse gas emissions. "Relative decoupling" of growth from environmental degradation is of course common, as growth becomes less resource and carbon-intensive and as a larger portion of the waste is recycled: thus, between 1960 and 2000, "decarbonization" occurred at a rate of 1.28% per year, although the rate has significantly decreased since then. "Absolute decoupling", in contrast, where efficiency gains increase faster than total output, occurs only exceptionally. The evolution of the pattern of greenhouse gas emissions is typical: except for rare periods of economic downturn, the reduction of volumes of greenhouse gas emissions achieved in certain jurisdictions is mainly explained by the fact that the accounting of emissions is territorial, based on what is produced and consumed within the territory, without taking into account emissions embedded in goods or services imported from abroad. In other terms, where it is claimed that absolute decoupling of growth from emissions has occurred, it is most often due to the accounting method used under the United Nations Framework Convention on Climate Change, and such apparent gains in high-income jurisdictions have been paired with a larger part of the goods consumed being imported, as pollution has been outsourced to other countries (generally, resource-rich and poorer) (Jackson, 2017: chap. 5). That "green growth" thus conceived as an illusion has been most recently confirmed by Hickel and Kallis (2019). Based on a careful examination of the empirical evidence on resource use and greenhouse gas emissions over a period of 60 years, these researchers conclude that the narrative of green growth is "politically motivated". Scientific facts that demonstrate that it is naïve to pretend that growth can be combined with a reduced ecological footprint are all too often ignored in the name of political expediency:

> The assumption is that it is not politically acceptable to question economic growth and that no nation would voluntary limit growth in the name of the climate or environment; therefore green growth must be true, since the alternative is disaster.

The focus on technology-driven solutions is one symptom of this broader delusion:

> Of course, we need all of the technological innovations we can get, and we need to gear government policy toward driving these innovations, but this will not be enough in and of itself.... [In] order for efficiency gains to be effective, we will need to scale down aggregate economic activity too. It is more plausible that we will be able to achieve the necessary reductions in resource use and emissions without growth than with growth.

The belief in technology as a magic bullet has other significant consequences. Reliance on the introduction of new technologies encourages States to reward and stimulate research and development programmes within firms (large firms especially, which can invest more in such programmes), to design such resource-saving technologies. This is typically done by granting such actors intellectual property rights on their inventions. This however may be counterproductive, for two reasons. First, while some innovations may be stimulated by the prospect of being awarded a patent, patents can also block further creation, so that the net effect on the progress of science and technology is in many cases negative. Actors who acquire a dominant position thanks to the monopoly rights they are recognized on their inventions soon shall dedicate their energy and resources to further restrict competition and discourage the arrival of new entrants on the market, rather than to speed up innovation (Bessen and Meurer, 2008; Boldrin and Levine, 2008: 4 and 10–11). Moreover, for firms to innovate, they generally must be able to build on innovations from others, which patents may obstruct: indeed, in the most technologically advanced sectors as in software production, pharmaceuticals, or the seeds industry, it is the need to overcome such "patent thickets" that explains the drive towards increased concentration of the industry (Heller, 1998). Finally, research teams at universities and in public research institutes working on ecological and social transition may be hampered in obtaining sufficient information about new innovations, as more and more essential innovations are fenced behind private intellectual property rights, especially in the life sciences. For instance, as shown in systematic surveys, researchers in bioengineering and biology are confronted with frequent denials to access research materials and restraints on publication and academic freedom (Reichman et al., 2016: 73).

Attempts to shape the development process by protecting intellectual property in the hope of stimulating innovation, moreover, leads to a form of development that is neither inclusive nor even conducive to wealth-creation. Indeed, the strengthening of intellectual property (IP) rights is not even justified by the narrow quest for economic growth. A recent review of 124 developing countries' IP rights frameworks, seeking to identify correlations with economic growth and innovation, concluded that growth has an even greater effect on strengthened IP protection than the opposite, implying that IP protection's impact on growth should primarily be seen at best as indirect, stemming from what the authors call a "placebo" effect: the *belief* that strengthened IP rights shall stimulate growth (rather than the direct contribution of IP rights to favouring technology imports and innovation) has the virtues of a self-fulfilling prophecy (Gold et al., 2017). And whereas strong IP rights protection has often been presented as a condition for the transfer of technologies through investment flows (i.e., firms owning the technologies would be reluctant to invest where their IP rights would not be adequately protected); in fact, the real determinants of investment are the size of markets and the quality of the infrastructure and of the institutional framework: strong IP rights protection will not attract investors if these conditions are not present, and once these conditions are present, the weakness of IP rights protection would not appear to constitute a major obstacle (Baker et al., 2017: 30). It remains true, of course, that in knowledge-based economies, growth increasingly relies on access to technologies and knowledge, and that inventors deserve to be reasonably rewarded for their investment. The continued strengthening of IP rights, however, is not the right tool to stimulate innovation further: it results, instead, in rents that increase the market dominance of the incumbents, and discourages healthy competition; and while being rewarded to innovate, the dominant actors shall in fact have gradually fewer incentives to innovate, since the dominant position they occupy makes this less necessary for them.

For our purposes, however, the main concern is that technological innovations designed by a small number of firms benefiting from a set of incentives (including strong IP rights to reward them for their inventions) cannot be a substitute for a more ambitious understanding of the ecological transition, which also encourages behavioural changes. In that regard, the impacts of the introduction of "clean" technologies may in certain instances be ambiguous, since a significant portion of the gains from the introduction of more efficient technologies is annulled by various "rebound effects" (Khazzoom, 1980; Brookes, 1990; Holm and Englund, 2009). We may distinguish three separate rebound effects. First, a "substitution effect" occurs where increased efficiency in production methods, allowing for instance for the reduction of the amount of energy per output (per distance travelled, per surface heated, per volume produced), lead to an increase in consumption because the good or the service will be cheaper. Second, efficiency-enhancing technologies may result in a "revenue effect", where the savings allowed by the improved efficiency of certain equipment and services can lead to increased consumption of other products. Third and finally, the dissemination of such technologies may cause what might be called a "licensing effect", as consumers who (thanks to technological advances) reduce their footprint in certain domains shall allow themselves to increase that footprint in other sectors: studies show, for instance, that carbon credit schemes have led to an increase in airline traffic, because people who otherwise might feel guilty feel that they can ignore the environmental impacts of their travels (Khan et al., 2010; Clot et al., 2014), and we all know of people around us who travel by air to exotic destinations for their holidays because they drive a hybrid car during the year, a phenomenon psychologists call the "compartmentalization effect" (Clot et al., 2014).

Betting on the introduction of new technologies, however "greener" or "cleaner", to achieve the ecological transition, may therefore not only reinforce further the position of economic actors who are already dominant; it may also discourage the very behavioural changes we should seek to promote. Indeed, the various rebound effects are important enough to cast doubt on the Ehrlich/Holdren equation itself, which is incomplete in that it does not factor our lifestyles into the factors that determine our ecological footprint – from the most lavish and inconsiderate to the more sober and conscious. This is in part what led Peter Schulze, director of the Center of Environmental Studies at Austin College, to propose an alternative, by introducing behaviour (B), in addition to population growth (P), income levels (A), and technology (T), among the factors determining our ecological footprint. Schulze's equation (I (Impact) = P × B × A × T) (Schulze, 2002) is not only more realistic; it also encourages us to think about innovation as not only technology-driven but also as comprising social innovations, leading to lifestyle changes.

One can get an idea of the relative importance of the behavioural change dimension in Schulze's equation as compared to the technological dimension by looking at the scientific data gathered in the "Exponential Roadmap" for combatting climate change. The Roadmap was prepared by an international consortium of leading sustainability scientists led by the Stockholm Resilience Centre. It aims to quantify the respective impacts of technological, behavioural, and economic changes on combatting climate change (with a very modest target of halving emissions by 2050). And the results are striking. While energy provision choices account for 35% of the contributions needed to decreasing emissions, the other changes required are in large part behavioural: at least 50% of the main changes that should occur to decrease emissions are related to behavioural changes, such as shifts in mobility choices, food choices, agricultural practices, and recycling (Falk et al., 2019: 12–13).

Nor is this all. A third limitation to this view of the ecological transition is that, in order to make a significant contribution, the new technologies would have to be deployed at such a scale that many years shall be required before the current trends of resource depletion and rising pollution levels can be reversed. The older technologies are difficult to displace, for a number of reasons (EEA, 2019: 25–26). Because they have already been deployed at a large scale, they achieve economies of scale and result in network effects that allow them to be highly competitive, and to discourage, as a result, the emergence of "green" alternatives (Arthur, 1994). Investments in established technologies and associated infrastructures are "sunk costs", assets that must be exploited until they are fully depreciated, or losses will appear on the balance sheets of the companies owning such assets. Workers, and indeed whole regions, may depend on the jobs and economic returns from the old technology, so that rapid change will meet with strong resistance, both from the corporate interests involved and from wider segments of society. These different factors inhibiting change are magnified by the fact that specific technologies are combined with the emergence of networks and infrastructures (suppliers or repair parts, highways, gas stations, and garages for cars, for instance) so that the challenge is not simply to replace one technology with another (say, fuels-based thermic engines by electrical vehicles), but to transform the whole network and associated infrastructures. Finally, existing technologies go hand in hand with consumers' lifestyles and established routines, which can be very resistant to change, due to what psychologists and behavioural economists refer to as the "endowment effect" (Tversky and Kahneman, 1991; Kahneman, 2011: 289–299; Thaler, 2015: 12–19), or that is more commonly known as loss aversion, or "status quo bias".

The consequence of such inertia factors is that there often exists a significant time lag between the introduction of a new, "green" technology, and its ability to have a transformative impact at the scale required: 10–20 years would be required for the electric cars to replace the cars that are currently equipped with thermic engines using fossil fuels, and a generation at least would be needed to renovate all buildings in order to significantly reduce the amount of energy required for heating them (or for keeping them cool) (Bihouix, 2014: 72–74). We simply cannot afford that time.

Myth #2 That green capitalism and corporate social responsibility are the answers

A second myth is that green capitalism shall provide the answers to the environmental challenges we face, if only we create the right conditions for corporations to contribute to the transformation required. Socially responsible investment, after all, is a fast-growing industry. Consumers are increasingly making their choices based not on price and quality only, but also by taking into account sustainability concerns – including those related to the environmental impacts of production and to working conditions. Public entities are becoming aware of the potential role of public procurement in accelerating the transition towards sustainability (see, for instance, McCrudden, 2007; Morgan and Sonnino, 2008; EC, 2017). Companies are aware that, in order to attract or retain investors and consumers, and to be eligible for public contracts, they must adapt to these changing expectations. The Sustainable Development Goals themselves are strongly supportive of this shift. Under SDG 12, which is to "Ensure sustainable consumption and production patterns", Target 12.5 is to "Encourage companies, especially large and transnational companies, to adopt sustainable practices and to integrate sustainability information into their reporting cycle", and Target 12.6 is to "Promote public procurement practices that are sustainable, in accordance with national policies and priorities".

Indeed, the enlightened self-interest of companies, particularly large companies who have most reasons to care about their brand reputation, may converge here with changing social expectations.

In competitive and increasingly globalized markets, buyers may seek to differentiate their products by resorting to standards that serve a "signalling" function, allowing them to segment the market in their favour and, if possible, to reduce the pressure of competition (Spence, 1976; Mussa and Rosen, 1978; Vandemoortele, 2011). This quest for differentiation and for segmentation is a major factor explaining why, even in the presence of minimum quality standards imposed through public regulation, buyers may exhibit "voluntary overcompliance": in the agrifood sector, for instance, they shall opt for even more demanding standards, which will attract consumers who are prepared to pay a premium for an even higher level of safety (Vandemoortele, 2011, building on Arora and Gangopadhyay, 1995).

The potential contribution of the rise of corporate social responsibility since the 1980s and the growing concern for reputation in the business community for the shift to low-carbon, biodiversity-respecting societies should not be underestimated: the more economic power is concentrated, the more even a small number of major economic actors can make a difference across global supply chains. In this regard, the rise of human rights due diligence obligations not only in the operations of corporations but also across all their business relationships is particularly significant, particularly insofar as such human rights include environmental rights and rights on which livelihoods of local communities depend. It means, in effect, that the largest transnational corporations shall be more closely monitored, and that globalization of economic activity, which until recently has been encouraging social and environmental dumping as well as fiscal "optimization" strategies (leading to unhealthy fiscal competition between States, see Dagan, 2017), may gradually become an instrument for the betterment of the behaviour of corporate actors involved in large multinational groups or in long supply chains (Darcy, 2017).

Yet, there are limits to what can be expected from this evolution. First, the different channels through which companies can be incentivized to incorporate a concern for sustainability in their business practices shall work more or less effectively, depending on the type of company concerned and on the environment in which they operate. Not all companies are publicly listed, and not all need, therefore, to remain attractive to investors, particularly institutional investors, which now express concern for sustainability. Not all companies have reasons to fear the response of consumers, including in the most extreme form of a call to boycott, since not all engage in B-to-C operations – although this limitation is one that the emerging due diligence requirement should in principle help to overcome. Not all companies, finally, depend on public contracts, and therefore shall be affected by the changing role of public procurement – which now is guided not exclusively by the search for the "most economically advantageous" offer, but also by a concern for social and environmental sustainability (McCrudden, 2004, 2007).

Second, changes within the corporate world may largely annul any benefits that can be expected from CSR initiatives. Since the 1980s, companies have increasingly invested in strategies that maximize shareholder value, and that raise the levels of compensation of the top ranks of the corporate hierarchy (Epstein, 2005; DiPrete et al., 2010; Philippon and Reshef, 2013; Lazonick, 2016). The most common techniques relied upon to that effect include buying back of the company's shares in order to increase its market value; reorganizing value chains to favour disaggregation of the production process; outsourcing parts of the production to partners located in jurisdictions where labour is cheap and docile, and where environmental regulations are lax or underenforced; and resorting to price transfer mechanisms to reduce the tax liability of the corporate group. These strategies have been encouraged by the growth of financial markets, which now significantly dwarf the value created in the real economy, and they have in turn led to capital accumulation and the further increase of the weight of financial markets: it is this phenomenon of financialization, which has taken the shape of a positive feedback loop, that has led to the regular growth of bubbles in recent decades, and to increasingly unstable markets (Krippner, 2011). Moreover, companies now operate across global value chains, in an environment in which producers compete on a worldwide basis: this development, which digitalization, as well as the lowering of barriers to trade and investment, have greatly facilitated, is a significant obstacle for many companies in their quest for sustainability, at least as long as trade policies do not incorporate a concern for labour standards and environmental safeguards (De Schutter, 2015).

It is thus highly doubtful, in such a context, whether voluntary pledges shall make any significant difference. Where companies are rewarded for their good practices – where, in other terms, the "business case" for responsible business practices is strong –, CSR may pay; but in most cases, and for most companies, particularly those operating in the most competitive sectors, that shall not be the case until the business environment is significantly reshaped in order to create the right set of incentives (De Schutter, 2008).

Myth #3 That the State is best placed to help us out of our predicament

A third persistent myth about the transition is that societal transformation can be achieved by the State, provided its role as the
guardian of the public interest is reaffirmed. If only the State could
effectively take bold decisions without being hindered by the various counter-forces that it currently faces, according to this narrative, we should trust the central government to make the necessary
changes. At the heart of this idea, is a nostalgia about the classic idea
of the sovereign: the past couple of decades have witnessed a "de-
democratization" of the State, which has made it increasingly difficult for the governmental apparatus to regulate in the public interest
and has rendered this classic conception increasingly irrelevant. Such
"de-democratization" has its source in the global trend towards
devolution – the delegation of power to sub-national entities, regional
or local. It also results from economic globalization – the lowering of
barriers to trade and investment, facilitated by new technologies, by
the reduction of the costs of transport, and by the conclusion of free
trade agreements and investment treaties. It is encouraged, finally, by
the privatization of services or the rise of public-private partnerships.
These three developments work in combination, Dana Freeman has
argued, to create a situation in which the policy-making preroga-
tive of States "has been redistributed 'up' to the supranational level,
'down' to lower State levels and 'across' to the markets" (Freeman,
2017). Might countering these trends allow to re-establish the State in
its ability to transform society? Should we re-create the Leviathan, to
allow it to effectuate the massive changes that the current situation
requires?

Whether the concentration of power in the hands of the State constitutes an opportunity or a liability remains debated. Obviously, such
concentration of power may allow for robust programmes of social
transformation to be put in place, at the scale required in the present
situation: a strong State, it might be argued, is required in order to disrupt routines, to overcome the opposition of vested interests who have
no interest in change, and to maintain a focus on long-term objectives
(Eckersley, 2020). Indeed, as remarked by James Galbraith, free markets may be good as rewarding the most efficient solutions, but they
are unable to plan ahead, although societies need long-term visions to
ensure that the resources are invested not only to maximize immediate
gains but also to prepare for the future. Planning is required, in particular, to address the questions of

how much in the aggregate to invest (and therefore to save), the directions to be taken by new technology, the question of how much weight and urgency are to be given to environmental issues, the role of education, and of scientific knowledge, and culture. Decisions on these matters involve representing the interests of the future – interests that are poorly represented by markets.

(Galbraith, 2008: 165)

Markets, moreover, cannot be trusted to register the expectations and hopes of the weakest components of society and of future generations: they register, after all, *demand*, as expressed in the purchasing power of consumers, in proportion to their ability to pay. As Scitovsky famously quipped (1976: 8), markets are plutocracies: you get to vote on the allocation of resources in proportion to the money you can put on the table. Isn't the most urgent task, then, to reassert the primacy of democracies? Should we therefore not place our trust in States, that can take into account *needs*, as expressed by voters, rather than *demand*, expressed in purchasing power? Should we not replace the State in the central position it once had, to allow it to make change happen?

But there are counter-arguments to this narrative. We offer three arguments to justify our scepticism towards the idea that the "green State" can orchestrate the societal transformation required to combine environmental sustainability with social justice. The first argument concerns the co-optation of State power. Power that is concentrated is power that can be more easily captured: the economic elites and the large corporations can more easily translate their economic power into political influence, where decision-making is highly centralized. Indeed, confirming certain intuitions of public choice theorists (Buchanan and Tullock, 1962; Krueger, 1974; Zingales, 2017), recent studies have shed light on the considerable distortions powerful economic actors could introduce even in democratic decision-making. Martin Gilens and Benjamin Page, for instance, have illustrated how decision-making by elected representatives systematically favours large corporations – the economic elites –, betraying the expectations of ordinary people (Gilens, 2012; Gilens and Page, 2014); and while their empirical work is focused on the situation of the United States, where money plays a particularly important role in politics (see also Drutman, 2015), this is not an exceptional case. Lobbying in the EU, for instance, is a well-documented reality, and it has grown over the years, despite the establishment of a series of safeguard mechanisms (Coen, 2007; European Parliament, 2007). The phenomenon of corporate capture has gone global. It was the exception; it has become the rule (George, 2015).

The United Nations Conference for Trade and Development (UNC-TAD) flagship 2017 *Trade and Development Report* is one of the most significant recent contributions to the debate on the impacts of the capture of the political system by the most powerful economic actors. In a chapter titled "Market Power and Inequality: The Revenge of the Rentiers", the report argues that

> increasing market concentration in leading sectors of the global economy and the growing market and lobbying powers of dominant corporations are creating a new form of global rentier capitalism to the detriment of balanced and inclusive growth for the many.
>
> (UNCTAD, 2017: 119)

Abuses of a dominant position to extract a rent (a "surplus profit", representing the difference between the typical profits that should be expected and the actual profits made) have economic consequences: they estimate that for the top 100 firms, 40% of the profits made are the result of "rents", a percentage that have increased from 16% in the years 1995–2000 and 30% in the years 2001–2008. This increase is largely attributable to increased market concentration (10% of the world's publicly listed companies capture 80% of the profits) but also to the ability of the most powerful actors to shape the competitive environment to their advantage. What emerges, the UNCTAD writes, is "a vicious cycle of underregulation and regulatory capture, on the one hand, and further rampant growth of corporate market power on the other". This is a trap in which globalization, initially promoted by States, is now increasingly shaped by the international division of labour resulting from the strategies of transnational firms, strategies that States now are finding out they are hardly equipped to oppose (UNCTAD, 2017: 139). This imposes a major limitation to the ability of the State to promote a social and ecological transition: any measure that might reduce the profitability of investments under their jurisdictions shall either be challenged as a violation of investors' rights, or lead to a threat of outsourcing production, giving considerable weight to large firms in political decision-making.

Is the answer, then, to establish safeguards against the capture of government, by combining a recentralization of State power with the democratisation of central State decision-making, for instance by imposing strong prohibitions on the financing by corporate actors of electoral campaigns or by restricting lobbying efforts? This approach faces a number of problems. First, this would only constitute a very partial answer to the challenges associated with the "de-democratization" of the State referred to above: in a globalized world, in which market-based solutions are prioritized both for ideological reasons and in order to maintain a "competitive State" (Hirsch, 1995), a centralized State could be little else than a transmission belt for imposing the exigencies of the market across society. Second, however much desirable is may seem on paper, democratizing State power in a centralized setting reduces the democratic participation of the citizen to its limited role as a voter and shall lead politicians to act in accordance with the expectations of the median voter (Acemoglu and Robinson, 2000); and it is unclear, to put it mildly, that the median voter shall choose for the kind of lifestyle (sober, simpler, and with a reduced ecological footprint) that the pace of the degradation of the ecosystems requires. In fact, democracy in such a centralized setting, in which voters give a mandate to elected politicians to think and act for the people, without including mechanisms for a more regular and active involvement of citizens in contributing to collective choices, may appear as a recipe to focus on the most short-term and least sustainable solutions. Thirdly, the insistence on centralized solutions might discourage, rather than facilitate, territorial approaches, based on local experimentation, that align policy frameworks on the specific resources and motivations that exist within each eco-bio-region. Even in more inclusive forms of democracy, with institutionalized forms of consultation of labour organizations and public interest groups, such as in the Northern European models of consociational democracy, centralization is sometimes perceived as an obstacle to the organization of collective action at local and regional levels (Borowski et al., 2008; Nielsen et al., 2013).

There is a second, more structural reason why the State is poorly equipped to lead the ecological transformation of society. In order to provide the services the public demands, and to reduce inequalities by financing social protection, the State almost inevitably must encourage wealth creation. Historically, this has meant facilitating the expansion of trade, creating a "business-friendly environment" (a codeword for lowering taxes and regulatory burdens on corporations), and deregulating the labour market: these were in the past the preferred recipes for stimulating economic growth, which is necessary not only to allow the State to fulfil its functions but also to service the public debt – a concern that has gained in urgency since the crisis induced by the Covid-19 pandemic. This leads to the State and the market forming a condominium, in which each needs to other to survive and to make progress: "contemporary markets and States co-constitute each other", David Bollier and Silke Helfrich (2019: 285) write that while markets need the State to provide physical infrastructure, reliable institutions, and financial and human capital, the State in turn relies on markets for the creation of jobs, for the provision of low-priced goods and services that the population expects, and for tax revenues.

Some authors have concluded that, since States depend on private capital accumulation, they cannot be expected to support any form of development that will lead to degrowth (understood as a reduction of GDP per capita): Matthew Paterson, a leading political scientist on environmental issues at the University of Ottawa, considers that "a green State is... impossible, since the State as we know it and capitalism (for which accumulation is the basic premise) are historically and structurally co-existent" (Paterson, 2016: 6). In the same vein, Daniel Bailey has presented this as the environmental State "trilemma": it is impossible, he argues, at the same time orchestrate degrowth, to maintain the fiscal viability of the State, and to expand the environmental functions of the State (Bailey, 2015). These are not isolated voices: the scepticism around the idea of a "green State" is widespread, because of this dependency of states on the endless expansion of wealth creation.

Twentieth-century thinking saw growth, indeed, as a pre-condition for both the reduction of inequalities and the eradication of poverty, and the wiping out of environmental damage. We now require something else: a development model that takes seriously the interrelated challenges of social cohesion and environmental sustainability, by incorporating these concerns in the model of growth itself, rather than seeing them as an afterthought or a hoped-for byproduct. This is achievable, as one of us has argued in detail elsewhere, provided we invest in "triple-dividend" solutions that create jobs, ensure affordable access to essential goods and services, and at the same reduce our ecological footprint (De Schutter, 2020; De Schutter et al., 2021) – and we return below to the question of what real prosperity can mean in a post-growth world. The impossibility therefore is not logical. But it is political, and therefore still real. In theory, the State should be able to orchestrate a shift away from the dominant model of growth, which depends on an extractive relationship to nature and on the accumulation of wealth as a means to finance public services and redistributive policies; the Swedish scholar Robyn Eckersley is correct, in that regard, to note that

> States are better placed than any other actor or organisation to facilitate socio-ecological transformation given their powers to

regulate, tax, spend, redistribute, and procure and to perform these tasks in ways that are more or less responsive and accountable to citizens.

(Eckersley, 2020)

Nevertheless, the expectations of the public concerning access to consumer goods, and the resistance with which any radical reform of the tax structure is likely to meet (including the pricing of carbon at a high enough level to bring about significant changes to the current patterns of production and consumption), makes us pessimistic about a transformation scenario based on State leadership alone.

Third and finally, the tools by which States can seek to encourage societal transformation are limited in range, and they are only partly adequate. Social psychology teaches us that injunctions imposed from above, in the way typical top-down fashion regulations are designed, have a limited ability to bring about deep and lasting behavioural change. Already in the 1960s, Jack Brehm – joined later by his wife Sharon, who transposed the theory to the clinical psychology setting – put forward "reactance" as a universal psychological trend of resisting any imposition that is perceived as restricting individual freedom (Brehm, 1966; Brehm and Brehm, 1981). It is this hypothesis that has led contemporary psychologists to explore the virtues of "self-determination", by which they mean the potential of behavioural change that results from equipping the individual with the skills, and allowing that individual the space to experiment, in order to ensure that such change shall correspond not to an imposition from above, but from a motivation from within – what they refer to as an "intrinsic" motivation (Ryan and Deci, 2000a, 2000b; Moller et al., 2006).

This distinction between "extrinsic" and "intrinsic" motivations – or, in common parlance, between an approach based on incentives (sanctions and rewards) and an approach based on persuasion (ensuring the individual adopts as his or her own the reasons to act that are also good for society) – is related in an important way to the ability for the State to effectively bring about a societal transformation that presupposes changes in individual behaviour. Indeed, the two main tools that States rely on – legal sanctions and economic incentives – share a common understanding of the individual. This understanding can be traced back to the rise of utilitarianism in the late 18th century, which sees the individual as an object to be influenced from the outside – a pawn to be moved on the chessboard. This is what Hannah Arendt referred to as the "substitution of behavior for action", which she saw as one characteristic of the modern age, and which the ascent of social sciences as "behavioral sciences" further strengthened: the aim of such sciences, she noted, is "to reduce man as a whole, in all its activities, to the level of a conditioned and behaving animal" (Arendt, 1958: 45). This is perhaps best illustrated by the 20th-century triumph of economics, which have been the "social science par excellence", the truly dominant "science of the State" (as the etymology of the word "statistics" betrays, or as the expression "political economy", as the science of economics was originally called, also alludes to): economics, indeed, "could achieve a scientific character only when men had become social beings and unanimously followed certain patterns of behavior, so that those who did not keep the rules could be considered to be asocial or abnormal" (Arendt, 1958: 42).

The antidote to such State-centred behaviourism is action; the antidote to such technocratic depoliticization is politics. This is why we would submit that the enabling State should not simply be a democratic State, one in which the rulers are accountable to the people; it should be a State in which power is distributed across the community, and in which therefore the democratic requirement applies not to the State only, but to the whole of society. The enabling State requires a high-energy democracy, one that is not limited to periodic elections, but that allows for the permanent involvement of ordinary women and men in collective decision-making. This is quite different to, and potentially incompatible with, the idea of giving the State a mandate to impose change from "above".

Myth #4 That bottom-up initiatives, led by ordinary people, are a substitute for both the State and the market

Since the turn of the millennium, but especially since 2007–2008, an impressive string of citizens-led initiatives to accelerate the ecological transition has developed: indeed, the spread of such initiatives is such that various authors have described it as a "revolution" (Church and Elster, 2002; Manier, 2012). The forms are highly varied (NESTA, 2009; McCarthy, 2010; Klein, 2010). They include community energy projects (Poize and Rüdiger, 2014; Seyfang et al., 2014), community vegetable gardens, community-supported agriculture recreating direct links between farmers and "eaters" (Seyfang, 2006), various forms of car-sharing, furniture-recycling social enterprises, social groceries, community composting schemes or the creation of local currencies, to name but a few. The expansion of these initiatives has been encouraged by the Transition Towns movement, now renamed Transition Network, launched in 2007 in the English town of Totnes by Rob

Hopkins and others (Hopkins, 2008, 2010). It has been encouraged by or through networks such as the International Council for Local Environmental Initiatives (ICLEI – Local Governments for Sustainability), established in 1990 at the initiative of the UN Environment Programme and now connecting more than 1,750 local and regional governments committed to sustainable urban development.

The growth of local, community-driven change for sustainable development has gone hand in hand with a renewed interest in social innovations as an instrument for social change. The concept itself is not new, of course: in fact, whereas the expression "technological innovation" only appeared in the 1930s, the idea of "social innovation" was already in use in the 19th century (Moulaert and MacCallum, 2019: 4). Its revival in contemporary discourse is nonetheless remarkable. It may be explained by a certain disillusionment with the bureaucratization of the welfare State, typical of the quest for individual autonomy of the 1960s and 1970s – in reaction to what critical theorists such as Herbert Marcuse called the risk of "unidimensionalization of man". The contemporary interest in social innovation is therefore ambiguous from the start. The most common advocacy for social innovation is that with the retreat of the Welfare State brought about by neoliberalism, other solutions must be found, which provide to individuals, either through the social and solidarity economy, or by the reconstitution of social links within the local community, the kind of support the State is not anymore, it seems, able to ensure. State-led interventions and social innovations developed "bottom-up" by communities have therefore often been contrasted to one another: as a result, although there are important exceptions (for instance, Oosterlynck et al., 2013, 2020), the role of the State in supporting social innovations has been neglected.

Community-led social innovations are more than a tool to fill the gap left open by the retreat of the State. They bring about a number of benefits to the communities concerned, including jobs creation; the creation of new, local markets in which local small businesses have greater chances of succeeding (this is a key aspect, in particular, of the introduction of alternative community currencies as well as of the short food chains); and the provision of services or goods that may be more affordable for households living on tight budgets (think for instance of repair cafés, or local exchange systems in which neighbours trade services between them, or of sharing or donating initiatives). These benefits to the local community appear to play a significant role in the motivations of the individuals investing in transition initiatives. This is illustrated by the results of a survey conducted in February 2009, during the early stage of the Transition Towns movement.

Gill Seyfang collected 74 responses received from the coordinators of the Transition initiatives in the UK (which at the time were 94). To the question of how they would rank the priorities of the transition initiative they were involved in (on a scale going from 0 (least important) to 5 (most important)), "building local self-reliance" achieved the highest score, ranking above "preparing for 'peak oil'" and "tackling climate change", although these latter two objectives have since the start been cited by its initiators as central to the Transition movement. Figure 2.1 summarizes the results of the survey.

It is perhaps equally significant that "community-building" scores so well in the survey. For those who dedicate their time and energy to launching and maintaining such citizens-led initiatives, in addition to the acquisition of new skills and the sheer pleasure of feeling empowered to design your own solutions at the local level (the same 2009 survey notes that, by the time of the survey, a third (32.9%) of the Transition initiatives covered had launched 'reskilling' projects, intended to facilitate the acquisition of "practical skills for everyday life" (Seyfang, 2009: 6)), the building of social links is one of the most often cited benefits expected from joining a transition initiative. Indeed, these are the source of "intrinsic motivations" amongst participants, who see value in investing in collective action quite apart from the question of whether or not the initiative shall contribute in any meaningful way to the professed end objective (such as building a circular economy, strengthening local resilience, or accelerating the shift to clean energy).

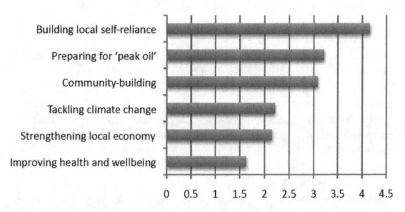

Figure 2.1 Most important motivations of actors of the Transition Towns movement in the UK.

Source: Seyfang (2009).

In that sense, local-level, citizens-led initiatives may be seen as a "counter-movement", a reaction to the significant erosion of "social capital" in the 1980s and 1990s. The expression is used here in the meaning it was given by Robert Putnam in *Bowling Alone*, his best-selling book of 2000. By "social capital", Putnam meant the social cement – trust, and social norms of reciprocity – that gives strength to social networks and favour collective action (Putnam, 2000; see also, on social isolation in America, measured by the proportion of people who have no confidence, McPherson and Smith-Lovin, 2006).

The phenomenon of social capital erosion documented by Putnam is certainly not specific to the United States, and it is now broadly acknowledged that loneliness, its key indicator, has serious consequences not only for individuals' well-being but also for their health and the economic stability of wider society. The association between the weakness of social relationships and mortality risk is perhaps the most striking. A famous meta-study presented in 2010 by Julianne Holt-Lunstad and her co-authors, based on an analysis of 148 studies that provided data on individuals' mortality as a function of social relationships (covering a total of 309,849 participants), arrived at the conclusion that "people with stronger social relationships had a 50% increased likelihood of survival than those with weaker social relationships": the "odds ratio" was a significant 1.5, which means that "by the time half of a hypothetical sample of 100 people has died, there will be five more people alive with stronger social relationships than people with weaker social relationships" (Holt-Lunstad et al., 2010). This, the authors note, places social isolation as a risk factor that is more important than better-understood factors such as obesity or lack of physical activity, and that is equivalent to smoking. Their conclusion: "Social relationship-based interventions represent a major opportunity to enhance not only the quality of life but also survival" (Holt-Lunstad et al., 2010). Many medical innovations to date have extended life expectancy, but sometimes at the expense of quality of life, and typically without much concern for maintaining and enhancing social links: another generation of innovations is required.

Indeed, in the United Kingdom, the loss of social capital has been recognized as such a major societal problem, with serious health and economic impacts, that a specific parliamentary inquiry was led on the issue. The Jo Cox Commission on Loneliness established to that effect defined loneliness as "a subjective, unwelcome feeling of lack or loss of companionship, which happens when we have a mismatch between the quantity and quality of social relationships that we have, and those that we want". It presented estimates according to which the impacts of loneliness were equivalent (as a measure of the toll on the individual's health) to smoking 15 cigarettes per day, and cost the British economy £32 billion per year. In its final report of December 2017, the Commission recommended among other measures to create an "innovation and spread fund", which they saw as fulfilling the following functions:

> stimulate innovation in solutions to loneliness across all ages, backgrounds and communities; provide seed funding for communities in need to come together to develop self-sustaining community activities which enable people to connect; scale-up and spread promising approaches to reaching out to isolated lonely individuals, offering practical and emotional support to overcome the barriers to reconnection – including community navigators and connectors, social prescribing schemes etc.
>
> (Jo Cox Commission on Loneliness, Final Report, 2017: 18)

Stimulating social innovation at community level may help combat loneliness or social isolation (the two, though not identical in their definitions, closely overlap). This is desirable in its own right. But it also can be a powerful tool for societal transformation. Indeed, there is broad evidence that changes in behavioural patterns are greatly facilitated by people doing things together, at the local level, within communities that share certain social norms and to which the individual aspires to belong. This is why, when – under the Labour government led at the time by Prime Minister Tony Blair – the United Kingdom adopted its 2005 Sustainable Development Strategy, it noted that

> one of the messages of the research is that sustainable development often works best when driven by people working together. We can learn and change our behaviour more effectively in groups: Community groups can help tackle climate change, develop community energy and transport projects, help minimise waste, improve the quality of the local environment, and promote fair trade and sustainable consumption and production.
>
> (UK Government, 2005: 27)

To maximize the potential of community action, the strategy continued, there is a need to strengthen the capacity of local communities: in particular, "better co-ordination is... needed within the voluntary and community sector and between national and local levels"

(UK Government, 2005: 28). A specific strategy, called *Community Action 2020 – Together We Can*, was designed to that effect. There is nothing unusual in the UK's approach. Indeed, governments in all world regions are gradually starting to acknowledge the potential for change that resides in community-led action at the local level. The June 1992 Rio Earth Summit (officially called the UN Conference on Environment and Development) already had adopted Agenda 21, a 350-pages long plan of action aimed at involving local governments in sustainable development. The document, which 178 participating governments approved at the Summit, includes under the heading "Empowering communities" (para 3.7.), the following commitment:

> Sustainable development must be achieved at every level of society. Peoples' organizations, women's groups and non-governmental organizations are important sources of innovation and action at the local level and have a strong interest and proven ability to promote sustainable livelihoods. Governments, in cooperation with appropriate international and non-governmental organizations, should support a community-driven approach to sustainability, which would include, inter alia:

> a   Empowering women through full participation in decision-making;
> b   Respecting the cultural integrity and the rights of indigenous people and their communities;
> c   Promoting or establishing grass-roots mechanisms to allow for the sharing of experience and knowledge between communities;
> d   Giving communities a large measure of participation in the sustainable management and protection of the local natural resources in order to enhance their productive capacity; e. Establishing a network of community-based learning centres for capacity-building and sustainable development.

Thus, the convergence of the local, of community-driven action, and of social innovation as a tool for sustainable development, is not recent. What does appear more remarkable since the past turn of the millennium, however, is that local communities have sought to take action without waiting for the initiative to come from governments: they are imaginative enough, or perhaps too impatient, to delay action further.

Whether this potential of societal transformation shall be fully tapped in the future is another issue. We believe that, unless a supportive environment is created, nurturing these citizens-led initiatives, this considerable potential may be wasted. First, these initiatives are led by volunteers, who dedicate their free time to making them work, often without much recognition beyond the circle of the other individuals involved, and of course, without any monetary compensation. For many such initiatives, simply surviving is a challenge. Even leaving aside the significant amount of energy spent on maintaining the initiative alive (as opposed to developing it to scale), this is a source of fragility that may explain why many such experiments are short-lived:

> First, they fail to develop robustness and resilience to shocks like funding cuts, key people leaving, turnover of volunteers, burnout of activists, shifts in government policy. Second, short-lived initiatives frequently leave no formally documented institutional learning. The skills and learning are tacitly held within people, rather than being consolidated in readily accessible forms.
>
> (Seyfang and Smith 2007: 596)

For the individuals involved in community-led initiatives, the most important limiting factor may be time. Tezcan Mert-Cakal and Mara Miele found that "insufficient human capital" (the lack of volunteers or members) was the most significant challenge reported by the initiators or community-supported agriculture (CSA) schemes in Wales in the UK (Mert-Cakal and Miele, 2020). In her research on the growth of alternative food systems, Paula Fernandez-Wulff interviewed over 100 actors of alternative food systems in specific localities of Belgium, Germany, Italy, Japan, Spain, and the United States – including in particular actors involved in the Transition Network, in Slow Food convivia, in urban agriculture or urban vegetable gardens projects, in the establishment of short food chains, or in community organisations. She asked them what were the main obstacles they encountered in deepening their participation. Figure 2.2 summarizes the results: time scarcity, more even than a lack of financial support, is listed overwhelmingly as the chief obstacle (Fernandez-Wulff, 2018: 91).

A second major obstacle to the diffusion of citizens-led social innovations is that the logic of such innovations is different from, and in some respects even the opposite of, the profit-seeking logic that is dominant on the market. Gill Seyfang and Adrian Smith provide an apt formulation of the resulting challenge: "how best to reward and encourage innovative behaviour at the grassroots – given that

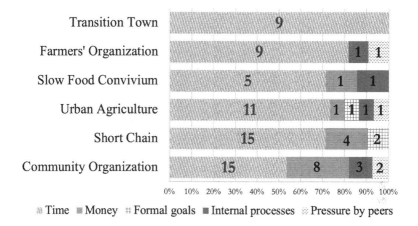

Figure 2.2 Obstacles cited by actors in alternative food systems.
Source: Fernandez-Wulff (2018).

rent-seeking behaviour is not the primary motivation" (Seyfang and Smith, 2007: 599)? Or, put differently: how to stimulate collective action in the long run, where classic economic incentives not only may not suffice, but could even have counter-productive effects, crowding out motivations for pro-social and pro-environmental behaviour that are more altruistic in nature? Whereas economic viability is arguably a condition for the initiative to be maintained beyond the initial formative years, steering the initiative towards profit-making, in order to attract a potential investor and to professionalize it, may dry up the very energy, from the ordinary men and women that launched the project, that allowed it to function. This is one reason why promoting the social and solidarity economy is so important: non-profit economic models are much better adapted to support citizens-led social innovations, allowing a much better "fit" between the two.

This may be seen as one specific illustration of the dilemma between co-optation and subversion. We explore this dilemma later, in a chapter in which we ask how niche innovations relate to the reform of the mainstream socio-technical regime: whereas citizens-led social innovations (or the most successful segments thereof) can be transformed into profitable businesses, attracting the interest of traditional investors and "start-uppers", this "success" may be very costly, leading in practice, in almost all cases, to a complete disappearance of the empowering component of the initiative; in contrast, we explain below that social and solidarity economy models may more easily provide a channel for the broader diffusion of the social innovation, without betraying its initial inspiration.

In sum, citizens-led social innovations provide important benefits to the participants themselves as well as to the local communities whose social fabric they serve to strengthen – and that alone should be a reason enough to justify such initiatives being supported. As a tool for society-wide transformation, however, they face important limitations. Their potential can only be fully tapped if the environment in which they operate is redesigned, to enable such initiatives not just to survive, but to provoke a transformation process within the mainstream regime. This means providing the material and human resources needed for these initiatives to be allowed to experiment during their initial stage; and linking up these initiatives, during a second stage, to local social entrepreneurs, motivated by values other than profit-maximization, and to local public officials taking leadership on supporting an ecological and social transition, to ensure their long-term economic viability. Unless these conditions are created, the risk is that citizens-led social innovations testing new schemes to move towards low-carbon and resilient societies shall either be co-opted in the mainstream regime, as they shall be seen as new profit opportunities by new entrepreneurs, or invoked by public authorities as a pretext to justify disengaging from certain areas – from local composting facilities to food waste prevention and from supporting households' access to renewable energy to maintaining community gardens –, following the neo-liberal logic described above. Indeed, both may happen at the same time: in areas such as car-sharing practices or the development of short food chains through community-supported agriculture schemes, profit-driven enterprises have emerged, building on what were initially citizens-led initiatives, while public authorities may have perceived as less urgent the need to improve access to mobility solutions for low-income households or to support small-scale farmers.

Beyond the myths

None of the bullets described above is magic; none of these myths is credible. Technology-driven solutions to sustainability, however important their short-term benefits in reducing pollution and in improving resource efficiency, may lead to the further deskilling of society (Illich, 1971; Bihouix, 2014) and to the further strengthening of already dominant economic actors, who can afford to invest in research and development programs and shall pledge to do so provided they have access to large enough markets allowing them to achieve the required economies of scale. The financialization of the economy, in turn, together with the globalization of competition, imposes significant limits to what can be achieved through voluntary actions from companies under corporate social responsibility schemes.

As to State-led transitions, they involve a risk of capture by these same actors, and they likely would rely on tools – legal mandates and economic incentives – that would rob us of the potential for innovation through local experimentation, and that has a mixed record as regards their ability to bring about lasting behavioural change. Yet, community-led social innovations too face important limitations: to escape premature death, they generally find themselves forced to accept co-optation by mainstream economic actors, or to remain constricted to a marginal, "fringe" position, which does not allow them to create the real alternative they wish to provide.

The idea of the Enabling State emerges at the juncture of these semi-failures and potential risks. We imagine a State that does not satisfy itself with putting in place the right set of incentives to encourage green technological innovation, and with creating the regulatory and policy framework that rewards best CSR practices, in the hope of stimulating a "race to the top" between companies competing to attract socially responsible investment and to retain critical consumers: this, governments already are doing. We imagine a State that is more ambitious, but which is ambitious in its modesty: rather than a State that pretends to know, and that operates in a top-down fashion to impose a transformation from above, we propose a State that accepts to learn, by supporting local experimentation. Empowering communities, encouraging them to come up with their own solutions, connecting these solutions to the social and solidarity economy to ensure their economic viability, and finally to challenge the mainstream regime: such an Enabling State can only properly deliver on these promises if, in its decision-making processes, it is radically democratized, in order to bridge the gap between the governing elites and the governed, and between the expert knowledge of the technocrats and the lay knowledge of social actors.

References

Acemoglu, D. and Robinson, J. (2000). Why did the West extend the franchise? Democracy, inequality and the growth in historical perspective. *The Quarterly Journal of Economics*, *115*: 1167–1199.

Arendt, H. (1958). *The Human Condition*. Chicago: University of Chicago Press.

Arora, S. and Gangopadhyay, S. (1995). Toward a theoretical model of voluntary overcompliance. *Journal of Economic Behavior and Organization, 28*: 289–309.

Arthur, W.B. (1994). *Increasing Returns and Path Dependence in the Economy.* Ann Arbor: University of Michigan Press.

Bailey, D. (2015). The environmental paradox of the welfare state: The dynamics of sustainability. *New Political Economy, 20*(6): 793–811.

Baker, D., Jayadev, A. and Stiglitz, J. (2017). *Innovation, Intellectual Property, and Development. A Better Set of Approaches for the 21st Century.* Shuttleworth Foundation. Retrieved online: https://www8.gsb.columbia.edu/faculty/jstiglitz/sites/jstiglitz/files/IP%20for%2021st%20Century%20-%20EN.pdf

Bessen, J. and Meurer, M.J. (2008). *Patent Failure: How Judges, Bureaucrats, and Lawyers Put Innovators at Risk.* Princeton, NJ: Princeton University Press.

Bihouix, P. (2014). *L'âge des low tech.* Paris: Seuil.

Boldrin, M. and Levine, D.K. (2008). *Against Intellectual Monopoly.* Cambridge: Cambridge University Press.

Bollier, D. and Helfrich, S. (2019). *Free, Fair and Alive. The Insurgent Power of the Commons.* Victoria, British Columbia: New Society Publ.

Borowski, I., Le Bourhis, J.P., Pahl-Wostl, C. and Barraqué, B. (2008). Spatial misfit in participatory river basin management: Effects on social learning, a comparative analysis of German and French case studies. *Ecology and Society, 13*(1): 7. Retrieved online: http://www.ecologyandsociety.org/vol13/iss1/art7/

Brehm, J.W. (1966). *Theory of Psychological Reactance.* San Diego, CA: Academic Press.

Brehm, S. and Brehm, J.W. (1981). *Psychological Reactance: A Theory of Freedom and Control.* New York: Academic Press.

Brookes, L. (1990). The greenhouse effect: The fallacies in the energy efficiency solution. *Energy Policy, 18*(2): 199–201.

Buchanan, J.M. and Tullock, G. (1962). *The Calculus of Consent: Logical Foundations of Constitutional Democracy.* Ann Arbor: University of Michigan Press.

Church, C. and Elster, J. (2002). *The Quiet Revolution.* Birmingham: Shell Better Britain.

Clot, S., Groleau, G., Ibanez, L. and Ndodjang, P. (2014). L'Effet de compensation morale ou comment les bonnes actions peuvent aboutir à une situation indésirable. *Revue économique, 65*(3): 557–572.

Coen, D. (2007). Empirical and theoretical studies in EU lobbying. *European Journal of Public Policy, 14*: 333.

Commoner, B. (1972). *The Closing Circle: Nature, Man, and Technology.* London: Jonathan Cape.

Dagan, T. (2017). *International Tax Policy: Between Competition and Cooperation.* Cambridge: Cambridge University Press.

Darcy, S. (2017). 'The elephant in the room': Tax avoidance & business and human rights. *Business and Human Rights Journal, 2*: 1–30.

De Schutter, O. (2008). Corporate social responsibility European style. *European Law Journal, 14*(2): 203–236.

De Schutter, O. (2015). *Trade in the Service of Sustainable Development: Linking Trade to Labour Rights and Environmental Standards.* Oxford and New York: Bloomsbury/Hart.

De Schutter, O. (2020). *The 'Just Transition': Eradicating poverty within planetary boundaries.* Report submitted by the Special Rapporteur on extreme poverty and human rights to the 75th session of the General Assembly, UN doc. A/75/181.

De Schutter, O., Petel, M., Detroux, A. and Osinski, A. (2021). 'Building Back Better': Social justice in the green economy. *International Journal of Public Law and Policy, 6*(4): 346–367.

DiPrete T.A., Eirich G.M. and Pittinsky, M. (2010). Compensation benchmarking, leapfrogs, and the surge in executive pay. *American Journal of Sociology, 115*: 1671–1712.

Drutman, L. (2015) *The Business of America is Lobbying: How Corporations Became Politicized and Politics Became More Corporate.* Oxford: Oxford University Press.

EC (2017). *Public Procurement for a Circular Economy: Good Practice and Guidance.* Brussels: European Commission.

Eckersley, R. (2020). Greening states and societies: From transitions to great transformations. *Environmental Politics*, DOI: 10.1080/09644016.2020.1810890.

EEA (2019). *Sustainability Transitions: Policy and Practice.* European Environment Agency Report No. 09/2019.

Ehrlich, P.R. and Holdren, J.P. (1971). Impact of population growth. *Science, 171:* 1212–1217.

Epstein, G.A. (2005). *Financialization and the World Economy.* Cheltenham: Edward Elgar Publishing.

European Parliament. (2007). *Lobbying in the European Union.* Directorate General Internal Policies of the Union, PE 393.226.

Falk, J., Gaffney, O., Bhowmik, A.K., Bergmark, P., Galaz, V., Gaskell, N., Henningsson, S., Höjer, M, Jacobson, L., Jónás, K., Kåberger, D., Klingenfeld, T., Lenhart, J., Loken, B., Lundén, D., Malmodin, J., Malmqvist, T., Olausson, V., Otto, I., Pearce, A., Pihl, E., and Shalit, T. (2019). Exponential Roadmap 1.5. *Future Earth.* Sweden (September 2019).

Fernandez-Wulff, P. (2018). "Human rights, human agency: A study of social innovations' collective agency in the localization of social rights." (Ph.D. thesis unpublished, UCLouvain).

Freeman, D. (2017). De-democratisation and rising inequality: The underlying cause of a worrying trend. Working Paper 12, Department of Anthropology and International Inequalities Institute, London: London School of Economics.

34   *Obstructing myths*

Galbraith, J. (2008). *The Predator State. How Conservatives Abandoned the Free Market and Why Liberals Should Too.* New York: Free Press.

George, S. (2015). *Shadow Sovereigns: How Global Corporations Are Seizing Power.* Cambridge: Polity Press.

Gilens, M. (2012). *Affluence and Influence. Economic Inequality and Political Power in America.* Princeton, NJ: Princeton University Press.

Gilens, M. and Page, B. (2014). Testing theories of American politics: Elites, interest groups and average citizens. *Perspectives on Politics, 12*(3): 564–581.

Gold, E.R., Morin, J.-Fr. and Shadeed, E. (2017). Does intellectual property lead to economic growth? Insights from an improved IP dataset. *Regulation & Governance*, DOI: 10.1111/rego.12165.

Heller, M.A. (1998). The tragedy of the anticommons: Property in the transition from Marx to markets. *Harvard Law Review, 1*, 621–688.

Hickel, J. and Kallis, G. (2019). Is green growth possible? *New Political Economy*, DOI: 10.1080/13563467.2019.1598964.

Hirsch, J. (1995). *Der nationale Wettbewerbsstaat: Staat, Demokratie und Politik im globalen Kapitalismus (The Competitive National State: State, Democracy and Politics in Global Capitalism).* Berlin and Amsterdam: Edition ID-Archiv.

Holm, S.-O. and Englund, G. (2009). Increased ecoefficiency and gross rebound effect: Evidence from USA and six European countries 1960–2002. *Ecological Economics, 68*(3): 879–887.

Holt-Lunstad, J., Smith, T.B. and Layton, J.B. (2010). Social relationships and mortality risk: A meta-analytic review. *PLoS Med, 7*(7): e1000316. DOI: 10.1371/journal.pmed.1000316.

Hopkins, R. (2008). *The Transition Handbook: From Oil Dependency to Local Resilience.* Totnes, UK: Green Books.

Hopkins, R. (2010). *What Can Communities Do?* Santa Rosa, CA: Post Carbon Institute.

Illich, I. (1971). *Deschooling Society.* London: Calder and Boyers Ltd.

Jackson, T. (2017). *Prosperity without Growth: Foundations for the Economy of Tomorrow.* London: Routledge.

Jo Cox Commission on Loneliness. (2017). *Combatting Loneliness One Conversation at a Time. A Call To Action.* Final Report. Retrieved online: https://www.ageuk.org.uk/globalassets/age-uk/documents/reports-and-publications/reports-and-briefings/active-communities/rb_dec17_jocox_commission_finalreport.pdf

Kahneman, D. (2011). *Thinking, Fast and Slow.* New York: Farrar, Straus & Giroux.

Khan, U., Dhar, R. and Schmidt, S. (2010). *Giving Consumers License to Enjoy Luxury.* MIT Sloan Management Review. Retrieved online: http://sloanreview.mit.edu/the-magazine/2010-	spring/51310/giving-consumers-license-to-enjoy-luxury/

Khazzoom, J.D. (1980). Economic implications of mandated efficiency standards for household appliances. *The Energy Journal, 1*: 21–40.

Klein, J.-L. (2010). Introduction: Social innovation at the crossroads between science, economy and society. In: Moulaert, F. (eds.). *International Handbook on Social Innovation: Collective Action, Social Learning and Transdisciplinary Research*: 9–12. Cheltenham: Edward Elgar Publishing.

Krippner, G.R. (2011). *Capitalizing on Crisis*. Cambridge, MA: Harvard University Press.

Krueger, A.O. (1974). The political economy of the rent-seeking society. *American Economic Review*, *64*(3): 291–303.

Lazonick, W. (2016). The value-extracting CEO: How executive stock-based pay undermines investment in productive capabilities. Working Paper No. 54, Institute for New Economic Thinking (INET), Oxford.

Manier, B. (2012). *Un million de révolutions tranquilles. Comment les citoyens changent le monde*. Paris: Les Liens qui libèrent.

McCarthy, M. (2010). *The Ecology of Innovation*. London: RSA.

McCrudden, C. (2004). Using public procurement to achieve social outcomes. *Natural Resources Forum*, *28*: 257–267.

McCrudden, C. (2007). *Buying Social Justice*. Oxford: Oxford University Press.

McPherson, M. and Smith-Lovin, L. (2006). Social isolation in America: Changes in core discussion networks over two decades. *American Sociological Review*, *71*: 353–375.

Mert-Cakal, T. and Miele, M. (2020). 'Workable utopias' for social change through inclusion and empowerment? Community supported agriculture (CSA) in Wales as social innovation. *Agriculture and Human Values*, *37*: 1241–1260.

Moller, A.C., Ryan, R.M. and Deci, E. (2006). Self-determination theory and public policy: Improving the quality of consumer decisions without using coercion. *Journal of Public Policy and Marketing*, *25*(1): 104–116.

Morgan, K. and Sonnino, R. (2008). *The School Food Revolution: Public Food and the Challenge of Sustainable Development*. London and Washington, DC: Earthscan.

Moulaert, F. and MacCallum, D. (2019). *Advanced Introduction to Social Innovation*. London: Edward Elgar Publ.

Mussa, M. and Rosen, S. (1978). Monopoly and product quality. *Journal of Economic Theory*, *18*: 301–317.

NESTA. (2009). *People-Powered Responses to Climate Change: Mapping Community-led Proposals to NESTA's Big Green Challenge*. London: NESTA.

Nielsen, H.Ø., Frederiksen, P., Saarikoski, H., Rytkönen, A.M. and Pedersen, A.B. (2013). How different institutional arrangements promote integrated river basin management. Evidence from the Baltic Sea Region. *Land Use Policy*, *30*(1): 437–445.

Oosterlynck, S., Kazepov, Y., Novy, A., Cools, P., Barberis, E., Wukovitsch, F., Sarius, T. and Leubolt, B. (2013). The butterfly and the elephant: Local social innovation, the welfare state and new poverty dynamics. Improve Discussion Paper No. 13/03, Herman Deleeck Centre for Social Policy, University of Antwerp, Antwerp.

Oosterlynck, S., Novy, A. and Kazepov, Y. (eds.). (2020). *Local Social Innovation to Combat Poverty and Exclusion: A Critical Appraisal.* Bristol: Policy Press.

Paterson, M. (2016). Political economy of greening the state. In: Gabrielson, T., Hall, C., Meyer, J.M. and Schlosberg, D. (eds.). *The Oxford Handbook of Environmental Political Theory*: 1–17. Oxford: Oxford University Press (online version).

Philippon, T. and Reshef, A. (2013). An international look at the growth of modern finance. *The Journal of Economic Perspectives*, 27(2): 73–96.

Poize, N. and Rüdinger, A. (2014). Projets citoyens pour la production d'énergie renouvelable: une comparaison France-Allemagne. Working Papers No. 01/14, Iddri, Paris, France, 24 p.

Putnam, R.D. (2000). *Bowling Alone: The Collapse and Revival of American Community.* New York: Simon Schuster.

Reichman, J., Uhlir, P. and Dedeurwaerdere, T. (2016). *Governing Digitally Integrated Genetic Resources, Data, and Literature. Global Intellectual Property Strategies for a Redesigned Microbial Research Commons*: 678. Cambridge: Cambridge University Press.

Ryan, R. and Deci, E. (2000a). Intrinsic and extrinsic motivations: Classic definitions and new directions. *Contemporary Educational Psychology, 25*: 54–67.

Ryan, R. and Deci, E. (2000b). Self-determination theory and the facilitation of intrinsic motivation, social development, and well-being. *American Psychologist, 55*(1): 68–78.

Schulze, P.C. (2002). I=PBAT. *Ecological Economics*, 40: 149–150.

Scitovsky, T. (1976). *The Joyless Economy: The Psychology of Human Satisfaction.* Oxford and New York: Oxford University Press (1992 revised edition).

Seyfang, G. (2006). Ecological citizenship and sustainable consumption: Examining local food networks. *Journal of Rural Studies, 22*(4): 385–395.

Seyfang, G. (2009). Green Shoots of Sustainability. The 2009 UK Transition Movement Survey. University of East Anglia. Retrieved online: https://www.transitionculture.org/wp-content/uploads/green-shoots-of-sustainability.pdf

Seyfang, G., Hielscher, S., Argreaves, T., Martiskainen, M. and Smith, A. (2014). A grassroots sustainable energy niche? Reflections on community energy in the UK. *Environmental Innovation and Societal Transitions, 13*: 21–44.

Seyfang, G. and Smith, A. (2007). Grassroots innovations for sustainable development: Towards a new research and policy agenda. *Environmental Politics, 16*(4): 584–603.

Spence, M. (1976). Product differentiation and welfare. *American Economic Review, 66*: 407–414.

Thaler, R. (2015). *Misbehaving: The Making of Behavioural Economics.* London: Penguin Books.

Tversky, A. and Kahneman, R. (1991). Loss aversion in riskless choice: A reference-dependent model. *Quarterly Journal of Economics, 106*: 1039–1061.

UK Government. (2005). *Securing the Future. The UK Government Sustainable Development Strategy.* Cm 6467. London: HMSO.

UNCTAD (2017). *Beyond Austerity: Towards a Global New Deal. Trade and Development Report 2017.* Geneva: United Nations Conference on Trade and Development.

Vandemoortele, T. (2011). When are private standards more stringent than public standards? Discussion Paper 296/2011, LICOS Centre for Institutions and Economic Performance, Leuven: KULeuven.

Zingales, L. (2017). Towards a political theory of the firm. New Working Paper Series No. 10, Stigler Center for the Study of the Economy and the State, University of Chicago, Chicago, IL.

3 How social innovations relate to societal transformation

Four scenarios

While we can achieve agreement on the general direction of progress, agreeing on how to get there may prove to be more difficult. We need a new sense of direction, in contrast to the current trajectory of our societies which evokes the opposite: the image of a self-piloting vessel heading towards an unknown destination. Having a long-term vision, however, without a clear understanding of the different steps required to realize it, risks remaining in the realm of utopia. We need both the vision and an idea of how to travel to the destination: not only an end goal but also a map to reach it.

Yet, there is no script to guide us. Moving towards socially just and environmentally sustainable societies – what Kate Raworth eloquently describes as the "just and safe space" for humanity, which she famously pictures in the form of the "doughnut" (Raworth, 2013) – will require addressing a set of complex and interrelated challenges. Therefore, intensive social learning and societal innovation on a large scale will be necessary. Changes will be required at three levels: at the level of individual behaviour; at the intermediate level of the immediate environment of the individual (social norms and beliefs, organization of the relationship between work and private life, connectivity, access to public services, etc.); and at the level, finally, of the larger societal, organisational, institutional, and global biophysical level. We need not be simply an all-of-government approach to societal transition; we need a whole-of-society approach.

The agency of social actors is key to achieving this. Social actors are not only involved in individual social learning. They also collectively innovate and create institutions and norms that can, for various purposes good and bad, change the structure of the world they face. For instance, markets, as they are currently institutionalized, reward individuals who make economically rational decisions – in other terms, who adopt a utility-maximizing type of behaviour, whatever

DOI: 10.4324/9781003223542-3

the impacts on the outside world or the long-term consequences of all economic actors adopting this same behaviour.

The picture of human motivation conveyed by economists is not just a convenient fiction, allowing markets to be modelled as if individuals were determinate, calculating machines. It also shapes the establishment of markets, and it creates a strong incentive for individuals to behave in accordance with this description. The figure of the *homo economics* has gained, in time, the power of a self-fulfilling prophecy (Poteete et al., 2010: 221), especially as economics have come to occupy the position that all social sciences seem to aspire to: it is not by accident that the students of economics show less willingness to cooperate than the average person (Frank et al., 1993). Moreover, insofar as competitive markets are institutionalized on the basis of a profit-maximizing rationale only, they are designed to eliminate players who do not follow that norm of behaviour (Alchian, 1950). In contrast, economic life could be organized around institutions that support actors who act on the basis of pro-social and pro-environmental motives, thus bringing in new players that will act based on intrinsic motivations of a very different kind (Ryan and Deci, 2000). In that sense, there is a *co-evolution* between the behaviour of individual actors and the institutional frameworks they inhabit: just like individuals shape these institutions, they are shaped by them. Collective agency, therefore, on the one hand – the ability to reshape the institutions we inhabit – and the kind of conversion we expect individual actors to make in order to contribute to sustainable societies, on the other hand, are mutually supportive: both should advance together.

Because there is no single script, however, and because the kind of transition pathway that may work in one context (say, in a poor neighbourhood in Rio de Janeiro) is likely not to work in a different context (for instance, in the suburbs of Amsterdam), it would be unwise to settle on a single institutional model. The collective search for solutions that can trigger the change at the scale requires diversity, not uniformity. There is no single "best" solution, but rather a panoply of solutions that are more or less suited to different contexts. Indeed, even in particular contexts, the most promising solutions are best identified by combining a diversity of perspectives and by encouraging dissenting views (Servan-Schreiber, 2018). A more fruitful route therefore is to foster a wide range of models of change and of transition pathways from which societies can collectively shape new organizational, normative, and institutional contexts that will guide future action. In order to achieve this, we must tap into the considerable potential of citizens-led social innovations and mission-driven public and private entrepreneurship. This avenue for change is decentralized. It operates bottom-up. It is based on collective intelligence and on distributed and contextual knowledge, rather than on the idea that there exists one single pathway towards change that can be driven from the centre. The grassroots innovations which can provide a starting point for organizing such society-wide transformations include car-sharing and the shift to lighter modes of transportation, such as bicycles and walking, in the area of mobility; the development of vegetable gardens, of social or cooperative groceries, of community fridges, or of community-supported agriculture, in the area of food; the rise of people-owned cooperatives for the deployment of windmills or solar panels, in the area of energy production; and similar innovations that originate in ordinary people taking initiatives, without waiting for solutions to come from the State or from market actors (for overviews, see NESTA, 2009; McCarthy, 2010). Can such grassroots innovations make a difference at a societal level? Under which conditions can they be truly transformative, leading to what might be called regime change?

We may seek to answer this question by using the analytical framework and associated vocabulary proposed by the Dutch school of transitions (see Rip and Kemp, 1998; Geels, 2002; Geels and Schot, 2007; Kemp et al., 2007; de Haan, 2010; Grin, 2010; Rotmans and Loorbach, 2010). The framework distinguishes three levels, the combination of which (within what these authors call a "multi-level perspective") may explain socio-technical transitions (see Figure 3.1). The level of the societal *landscape* corresponds to factors such as the degradation of the ecosystems and the increasing pressure on resources, the diffusion of certain cultural models, or the ageing of society. These factors are exogenous insofar as they cannot be easily influenced: social actors therefore generally take them as given, and seek to adapt to the developments that the landscape imposes on them. The level of the societal *regime* refers to the existing (mainstream) system which we inhabit and which shapes our lives. It includes socio-technical components (the inherited technological pathways and infrastructures), socio-economic components (the organization of markets and the weight of dominant economic actors), socio-cultural components (social norms and habits), and socio-political components (the organization of governance), in particular. Finally, our third level is that of *niche innovations*: this refers to technological or social innovations that originate in certain (relatively protected) spaces, such as universities, start-up companies, or municipalities, that experiment with new ways of producing or consuming, with new business models, or with new technological tools.

The established regime is particularly difficult to displace. In part, this is due to the fact that its different components have co-evolved: they are the products of a shared, evolutionary process. Changing any single component is therefore difficult without also addressing the others, since the various components have grown to become mutually supportive, strengthening one another. This explains in part why the mainstream regime is generally quite resilient, resistant to change, and is strongly path-dependent in how it reacts to external pressures. The established routines of consumption and production are supported by facilitating infrastructures, which can only be replaced over a long period of time, and that – as long as they are in place – discourage the emergence of alternatives (see for instance, in the field of energy, Jacobsson and Johnson, 2000).

One major obstacle to a reform of the mainstream regime *from within* is the dominant weight of the incumbents. The dominant actors of the mainstream regime have often achieved significant economies of scale, on increasingly globalized markets in which brand recognition constitutes a major asset, and in which various network effects allow them to maintain their dominant position – so that even the threat of "virtual competition", from potential new entrants, will barely either discipline these dominant actors or force them to innovate (Clark, 1985; Stiglitz, 1987; Dasgupta and Stiglitz, 1988). To the extent that the dominant actors have sought to influence the regulatory framework in their favour, in typical rent-seeking fashion, or simply because that framework has been designed to encourage production increases for the growth of mass consumption society, the legal rules in place further favour that dominance. Finally, a positive feedback has emerged between the lifestyle choices that predominate in a wasteful, mass-consumption society, and the direction of technological development and infrastructure development (Shove, 2003). We continue to boast about the agility and flexibility of our market-based societies, which are meant to react to changes in demand and to reorganize their production processes easily. The reality is rather the opposite of this fairy tale: in fact, we face a formidable inertia obstructing any significant change, and the institutional repertoire we've been exploring until now has remained remarkably small.

If we consider grassroots innovations as "niche innovations" under this framework (for similar attempts, see Hoogma et al., 2002; Seyfang and Haxeltine, 2012; Bui, 2015; Hege, 2016), the question that emerges is: under which conditions can such innovations lead to a "breakthrough", or a reconfiguration of the regime? The mainstream regime is relatively inert and well equipped to resist change. At the

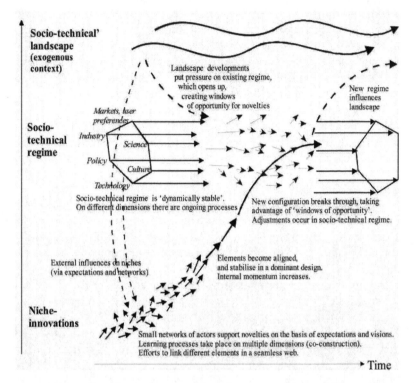

Figure 3.1 The multi-level perspective for the understanding of socio-
technical transitions.
Source: Geels (2002).

same time, each of the sub-systems of the mainstream is relatively autonomous, and therefore it cannot be excluded that certain changes
within a sub-system (in social norms, for instance, or following the
breakthrough of technological innovation) shall lead to a rearrange-
ment within the regime, and to the emergence of a new constellation
of factors. Moreover, the result of co-evolution of the different components of the system is not only a form of resilience to external shocks.
It also implies a strong interdependence between these components, so
that a threshold issue arises: whereas small changes to any of the components are easily absorbed by the system, once the change reaches a
certain level, it is the whole system that is forced to transform itself,
precisely because its various components depend on one another.

In order to better understand the conditions under which grassroots
innovations can lead to societal transformation, we examine four

distinct scenarios of change. Inspired in part by Geels (2011), though the typology we propose here differs from his own, we may rank these possibilities from the more modest or 'reformist' to the more ambitious or 'revolutionary'.

Scenario #1: collapse and reconstruction

At one end of the scale, is the scenario that sees a major crisis (sometimes referred to as a "collapse") as a condition for any significant change to occur: the deeper and the more sudden the crisis, the larger the opportunity.

This is a risky bet. The first question that arises is what we should do in the meantime. Perhaps paradoxically, the very fact that we think of "collapse" as being inevitable (and indeed desirable if it can accelerate the emergence of a different kind of society) may discourage the search for solutions in the short term, as such solutions would only delay the inevitable and, worse even, allow the existing mainstream system to buy more time. In addition, this 'revolutionary' path would require a crisis of a magnitude such that the mainstream economic growth model based on increased consumer spending would be wiped out entirely to be replaced by something else. The human costs likely to be involved until a new equilibrium is found may be high. Moreover, after the crisis, others will have their own "solutions". It is by no means certain that what shall emerge is a society built on conviviality and solidarity: it might as well be a society based on retrenchment and on growing inequalities. A well-documented example of this post-crisis capture by mainstream economic interests is the restoration of coastlines after the tsunami that hit South Asia in December 2004, where politicians were just as eager as those elsewhere to use the storm as an excuse to evict people and hand over land tenure to large resorts and large-scale tourism development: this is what Naomi Klein referred to as an instance of "disaster capitalism" (Klein, 2007).

The main reason why we shouldn't expect to build a new society on its "collapse" is because we can't wait. We can't wait, especially, until we run out of resources, particularly fossil fuels, before launching work on the societal transformation we need. The reason for this is that, as Bill McKibben (2007) once quipped, we shall be running out of planet before we will be running out of resources. The revolutionaries, in that sense, may not be impatient enough: it is likely that, by the time a collapse occurs of a sufficient magnitude, to force us to radically rethink our models of consumption and production, the damage caused to planet Earth will have passed the threshold of what is redeemable. (Indeed, some would remark: we have passed this threshold already. Whether or not this is true, we agree that we cannot wait for the final "collapse" to occur: the situation is too urgent to allow us to the luxury of waiting.)

Scenario #2: sociodiversity

The second scenario is one in which the grassroots innovations, without necessarily interacting directly with the mainstream regime, appear to create an alternative to the usual way of doing things. New production processes are tested; new motivations surface, different from the dominant profit motive; new lifestyles emerge. Political imagination is broadened as a result, and social norms are transformed. Instead of one dominant regime and "niche innovations" coexisting, what gradually emerges is a *sociodiverse* context, in which what was initially marginal may in time emerge as a new normal.

Sociodiversity should not be seen as an end in itself. It is, rather, a channel – our second channel – towards societal transformation. The social innovators act as norm entrepreneurs, more or less deliberately working to change social norms. *Norm bandwagons* develop: initially small shifts lead in time to broad changes, as a growing number of people join the norm; in time, they result in *norm cascades*, with sudden shifts in the dominant social norm (Kuran, 1995: 71–73; Sunstein, 1996: 909). Such shifts can be surprisingly quick. A study by a group of researchers from the University of Pennsylvania and the City University of London illustrated recently how a small minority can succeed in consciously changing the social convention that predominates in a community, even when this minority has no more social power or resources than the other group members, provided they manage to reach a "tipping point" leading to this change: the empirical trials conducted on such changes show that, over long time periods (i.e., beyond 1,000 interactions within the group), a committed minority of 25% shall almost certainly achieve the norm change, whereas for shorter time intervals (i.e., for fewer than 100 interactions), the "critical mass" required shall be between 20% and 30% of the group, and the predictability of change therefore is lower (Centola et al., 2018: see Figure 3.2).

The key point is this: there always exists a wedge, more or less important, between the preferences the members of a group *express* (either by professing to adhere to certain values or by acting in a certain way), and their "real" preferences (preferences that they hide from others because they feel that their opinions may be unpopular and thus costly to express publicly, and that are not translated into action because of the

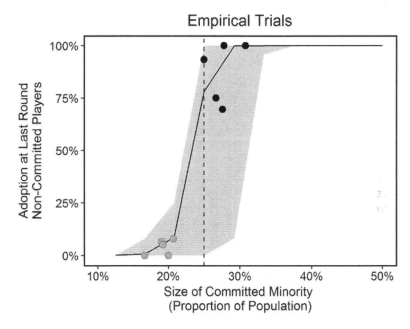

Figure 3.2 The ability of a "committed minority" to change a social convention.

Source: Centola et al. (2018).

This figure presents the final success levels from the empirical trials conducted by the researchers, who recruited 194 subjects from the World Wide Web and organized successive rounds of interactions to allow for the emergence of a social convention within the group (in stage 1), and then (in stage 2) introduced a variable number of "confederates" – a minority of individuals, the equivalent of 10%–30% of the whole group (percentage C, horizontal axis), committed to changing the social convention. The grey points in the figure indicate trials with $C < 25\%$; black points indicate trials with $C \geq 25\%$. The solid line in the figure indicates the theoretically predicted critical mass point with 95% confidence intervals (the grey area indicates 95% confidence intervals from 1,000 replications). The dotted line indicates $C = 25\%$. As the authors comment: "The theoretical model of critical mass provides a good approximation of the empirical findings. For short time periods ($T < 100$ interactions), the critical mass prediction is not exact (ranging from $20\% < C < 30\%$ of the population); however, over longer time periods ($T > 1,000$), the transition dynamics become more precise (solid line, 25)".

fear of marginalization). In such a context, the emergence of a group of people who put forward a different set of values or who act differently may encourage these "real" preferences to suddenly emerge, once the taboo surrounding them is lifted. Many revolutions develop precisely according to such a sequence: social innovations can constitute the triggering factor for such a broad transformation of social norms.

Even where such norm bandwagons do not form, the alternative provided by the niche innovation may encourage the actors of the mainstream regime, at the very least, to reflect on the limitations of their own worldview: institutions that were widely perceived as given and beyond critique suddenly appear for what they are – artificial creations, products of history, that can be unlocked. The growth of local exchanges of services provides one striking example. In such initiatives, members of the community trade services, based on the convention that each hour performed, whatever its market exchange value might be, is worth the same time-credit: whether you walk the dog of the neighbour, listen to the neighbour's complaints with a benevolent ear, provide a language lesson, or help him out in his relations with the administration, your time shall be computed identically. This *equal valuation of all productive labour* is in contrast with the conventional economy, but that, Seyfang and Smith argue, is precisely the point:

> Somewhat analogous to travelling through another country and culture, the experience causes us to reflect upon our home culture. The niche model might prove effective precisely because it draws contrasts. It could serve as a dialogical device for reflecting critically upon mainstream reforms. Stark contrasts between niche and mainstream, whilst making the translation of lessons from niche to mainstream difficult, can still provide a basis for critical reflection.
>
> (Seyfang and Smith, 2007: 595)

It is this reflective process that may be the start of a process of norm creation through which, gradually, a new equilibrium, based on a new set of social norms, may emerge.

This model of change faces a major impediment, however, which we have already referred to as loss aversion. To put it simply: we attach more value to what we already own than to what we might gain from change. In experimental settings, this generally applies to money or to objects, such as mugs in a famous experiment conducted by Amos Tversky and Daniel Kahneman (Tversky and Kahneman, 1991; Kahneman, 2011: 289–299; Thaler, 2015: 12–19). But it applies equally to established routines: usual ways of doing things, that we don't like to question or to see disrupted, despite the considerable benefits that, *post hoc* (i.e., once the transition is made), we might gain.

Preferences, it appears, are strongly baseline-dependent, and once the baseline changes, the preferences adapt easily. Gothenburg, Sweden's second-largest city, introduced a congestion charge in 2013: to reduce traffic during the busiest parts of the day, fees were introduced for the cars entering the city, that were higher during those most congested times (especially between 7 and 9 am and between 3.30 and 6 pm). A panel of 3,500 car owners of Gothenburg was surveyed before the scheme was introduced, and a follow-up survey was organized one year later, after the introduction of the scheme. Remarkably, although the attitudes towards the scheme were strongly negative before it was introduced (this of course explains why politicians fear imposing such a change, due to its unpopularity), the introduction of a congestions charge was positively evaluated in the second survey. The introduction of the new fee generally did not seem to affect the level of satisfaction with travel among those affected by the scheme, whether they decided to adapt by shifting modes of transport or reduce their commuting, or whether they decided to continue with the same commuting behavior, therefore paying the fee.

As noted by the researchers having conducted the study, this finding suggests that "although congestion charge schemes may be unpopular for several reasons the experienced effects need not be negative as people adapt" (Andersson and Nässén, 2016). The same is true for social innovations, such as new lifestyles that are more sober and simple. They may initially be perceived as losses. Once they become the new norm, however, they lead to a realignment of the preferences, and people may soon develop such an attachment to them that they will fear any return to the "earlier normal".

Scenario #3: co-optation

A third scenario according to which citizens-led social innovations can result in societal change is when the actors of the mainstream regime decide to co-opt the innovation in order to address a challenge they face, or to respond to the expectations of other stakeholders. A supermarket chain decides, for instance, to conclude an agreement with a charity to allow it to collect unsold food items nearing their sell-by date, thus at the same time responding to public concerns about food waste and reducing the costs of the treatment (by recycling or, more frequently, dumping in landfills). Here, the social innovation consists in charities linking supermarket stores with low-income families who are provided food aid. It is seen as providing an appropriate answer to the challenge the retail sector is facing, in a context in which a growing segment of the public is concerned about the levels of food waste (Papargyropoulou et al., 2014). Or – to take another example –, community energy projects might be supported by energy corporations, who may have an interest in partnering with such projects in order to improve their license to operate (whereas the opposition from local communities is a recurrent obstacle, for instance, to the deployment of wind farms), as well as to improve their "green" image (Seyfang and Haxeltine, 2012; Seyfang et al., 2014).

These examples illustrate the role which corporations may play in support of social innovations led by citizens. In other scenarios, public authorities may play a similar role: governments may amend the regulatory framework in order to allow such citizens-led initiatives to develop; local authorities may use public procurement schemes to reward such initiatives; they may contribute their technical expertise to allow the initiative to prosper.

The question that inevitably arises from such examples of co-optation is how to reconcile, or combine, the different value sets, or rationales, that coexist. Three separate value sets at least may be distinguished, corresponding to the triangulation characteristic of such scenarios – involving generally ordinary women and men, the "doers"; an economic actor; and a public actor, if not as an active participant, at least as an enabler adapting the regulatory and policy framework to facilitate the innovation.

The *citizens-led social innovations* are based on a decentralized logic, in which local knowledge and resources are mobilized in order to change the immediate environment, generally with a concern for sustainability as well as for the (re-)creation of social capital. As noted above, quite apart from the instrumental dimension of such community-led initiatives (i.e., the results they seek to achieve), such initiatives provide their own rewards for those engaging in them: they favour the learning of new skills, the strengthening of social links, and the sense of empowerment that is gained from designing solutions by counting on the community's own resources. The profit motive is generally absent, although the initiators may seek to ensure the economic viability of the initiative, to avoid it having to depend on the uncompensated work contributed by the participants.

Mainstream economic actors, in contrast, are motivated by the search for profits, especially when they are accountable to shareholders who expect a return on investment. They may also be attracted by the prospect of improving their understanding of a fast-changing market (i.e., of changing expectations of consumers); of becoming a more attractive company for prospective employees (who increasingly may value the possibility of dedicating some voluntary time to a non-profit enterprise); and of course, of improving their image in the general public. There is a risk, of course, that the forging of a partnership with a profit-driven company leads to distort the value set motivating the participants in the community initiative. Such partnership does bring certain rewards, however, since companies contribute what researchers from Erasmus University in Rotterdam call the "Five M's": Manpower, Money, Means, Media, and Mass (Roza et al., 2014). Teaming up with local entrepreneurs or larger economic actors, in some cases, may even appear as a condition for the long-term economic viability of the project.

Finally, *public authorities* operate with a view to promoting the public interest, and they shall in many cases be sympathetic to the idea of ordinary people taking initiatives to contribute to certain socially desirable goals. Depending on the level of governance concerned, however, their conception of the public interest may or may not correspond to the local economic development that citizens-led initiatives aim to promote: central authorities may in fact be sceptical about the professed need to stimulate local economic development, for instance at the level of one neighbourhood or one municipality, especially if they perceive this to be in conflict with the interest of other jurisdictions. Moreover, whereas public authorities may be eager to strengthen their legitimacy by joining forces with citizens' initiatives, they also may be concerned that empowering such initiatives may undermine their monopoly position with respect to the definition of the public interest, which they may see as an attribute of representative democracy: after all, isn't the very purpose of democratic elections to bring into power representatives whose role it is to define the goals of the community, and to make choices on its behalf?

The second pathway through which citizens-led social innovations may bring about change in the mainstream regime – which we call the scenario of co-optation – is therefore deeply ambiguous. On the one hand, co-optation may be seen as proof that the social innovation has been successful: after all, it has moved from its "niche" position to become "mainstream", and it has caught the eye of the incumbent actors, who control the mainstream regime, and now have turned to these social innovations in order to support it, learn from it, replicate it, and perhaps allow it to develop on an entirely different (larger) scale. On the other hand, however, this transformation entails a number of risks.

First, it may provide legitimacy to the mainstream regime, without bringing about the kind of structural change that would make it truly sustainable. This is what the accusation of "greenwashing" addressed at business actors, in the broad sense of the expression that includes the increased social legitimacy that accrues from working with communities (Seitanidi and Ryan, 2012), seeks to convey. But another risk arises with respect to the public authorities. It is that community action, in areas such as food provision, social inclusion, or the circular or functional economy (including by the recycling of waste or sharing initiatives), shall be seen by public authorities as a pretext for reducing their own investment in seeking to address certain issues.

The risk is well captured by the "Big Society, not Big Government" catchphrase coined for David Cameron by one of his key advisers, Steve Hilton, during the 2010 UK electoral campaign that led the Conservatives back to power after 12 years of Labour government: among the implications of this approach was a focus on encouraging individuals to donate money and time to community initiatives, in order to allow to cut social spending by government and to de-regulate (since stronger communities also are communities that, to a certain extent, can better self-police themselves; Halpern, 2015: 43 and 250–255). This was a failure: five years after the launch of the idea, it was barely referred to at all in official discourse, and an independent assessment considered that by 2015, "Fewer people feel they can influence local decisions, disenchantment with the political system remains widespread and communities are less strong" (Slocock et al., 2015: 6). One of the reasons for this failure is that, in its eagerness to encourage the voluntary sector to take over, the State reduced its support, at a time (following the major economic crisis of 2009–2011) when it was perhaps most needed. The same audit concluded in this regard that

> initiatives to encourage new sources of funding for voluntary sector organisations [were not] filling the void left by major cuts in state funding – particularly for smaller voluntary organisations, working in areas such as social services and employment, often with disadvantaged groups in disadvantaged areas.
>
> (Slocock et al., 2015: 8)

It is this risk also that various authors highlight when criticizing the role of food banks or charities justifying a rollback of the welfare State by providing support that compensates for the gaps in social protection (Allen and Guthman, 2006; Guthman, 2008); or that Nathan McClintock, drawing on his experience working on urban agriculture projects in the Californian town of Oakland, alludes to by noting that "some urban agriculture projects employ a neoliberal discourse of entrepreneurialism and self-help that shifts responsibility onto the shoulder of individuals and their communities" (McClintock, 2014).

A second risk is that co-optation may discourage the very actors who have invested in community action from continuing to do so, if they feel that they have been instrumentalized or disowned from the project: indeed, the very introduction of a concern for economic viability or for profit-making may crowd out the altruistic spirit in which the initiative was launched in the first place, thus removing a strong incentive for the initial participants – to do things differently, in a space protected from both a market logic and a bureaucratic logic, precisely in order to demonstrate that there is a real alternative to those dominant logics led by corporations or by the State.

The third and broader concern is that building an alliance with the private sector or the public sector, or both, may lead the routine ways of thinking and of doing of the incumbent dominant actors (corporations and State bureaucracies) to reaffirm their dominance, thus limiting the very possibility for truly imaginative alternative solutions to emerge. Indeed, based on their study of four different models of community-supported agriculture (CSA) schemes in Wales, Tezcan Mert-Cakal and Mara Miele concluded that for CSAs to become "workable utopias", they needed to involve actors from the mainstream regime – but they acknowledge that this raises the question of whether the CSAs can "preserve their alternative values" within such alliances (Mert-Cakal and Miele, 2020: 1256). The initiators of the citizens-led social innovation may understandably consider that sacrificing such values is a high price to pay, or an important risk to take, for the sake of being co-opted in the mainstream in order not to face premature extinction. They may thus seek to explore the fourth scenario.

Scenario #4: subversion

The fourth scenario is one in which the grassroots innovation neither remains marginal, nor seeks to be co-opted, but deliberately aims to transform the mainstream regime. In scenario #2, the innovators' sole ambition is to create a form of sociodiversity and thus to broaden the range of alternatives for society to choose from, as well as potentially leading to a change in social norms. In scenario #3, they seek the support of incumbents from the mainstream regime, with whom they form alliances or by whom they are co-opted. In our fourth scenario, they strategically design the social innovation in order to ensure that it shall be transformative of the regime.

What this requires depends of course on the context in which the innovation emerges, as well as on the particular constellation of actors that populate the regime. In general, for such subversion to succeed, a clear sense of direction shall be required: the innovators should be fully aware of what the end objective should be so that any concession made to ensure the short-term viability of the innovation shall not lead to renouncement. There may be tactical retreats, there may be concessions made, and progress may be slow at times; but there could be no permanent settlement until the mainstream regime's transformation is complete.

The difference between co-optation and subversion, between the previous scenario and this one, shall depend essentially on whether, as a result of the social innovation being nested within the mainstream regime, a new definition of the regime's end goals emerges. Together with other colleagues, we examined the conditions under which initiatives aimed at supporting local food producers in Belgium, by improving their access to markets, succeeded, or failed, to have a transformative impact (Bui et al., 2019). The movement towards improving the presence of "local products" in conventional retail markets was initiated by Carrefour, a major retailer, which – following meetings with farmers' representatives, which were necessary to rebuild trust between the parties – decided to offer local farmers specific (and especially favourable) marketing conditions: these farmers were allowed to enter into direct relationships with supermarket stores, thus sparing them the need to go through Carrefour's central purchasing department. This allowed the farmers to circumvent the normal process of price negotiation and to avoid other conditions such as back margins, payments for supply disruption, and recovery of unsold products, which otherwise exert strong pressure on prices and exclude small producers: according to the new arrangements, not only do the local producers define their own prices, they also are granted preferential treatment as regards delays of payment, and the duties of Carrefour stores are defined in a charter. Starting in 2012, the initiative was supported by two Belgian provinces, Liège and Hainaut, which allowed the number of contracted farmers to grow; and the success of the initiative was such that, after a few years, other major retailers followed the example of Carrefour.

These arrangements however did not lead to change in the governance of the food chain: the relationships between the food producers and the retailers still followed the conventional model, although the conditions applied were changed in order to better suit both parties' needs. Only two meetings per year were set up with the farmers: certainly not something that can be described as sharing power. In contrast, in another Belgian province (Walloon Brabant), a local action group (LAG) (funded by the EU's Common Agricultural Policy) teamed with the provincial authorities to create a new organization, "Made-in-BW", co-managed by the province, the municipalities members of the LAG, and representatives of small farmers, in order to create a new food hub. In addition to linking the local farmers with supermarkets, "Made-in-BW" supplied a diversity of stores, including a consumers' cooperative supermarket located in a working-class, multi-cultural neighbourhood, which aims to provide quality food to the most deprived: in fact, although it is economically viable, the project with the retailers is really seen by the initiators of "Made-in-BW" as a means to support, via other collaborations, the development of other schemes, including schemes competing with the very supermarkets that they team up with, which could not develop without this tool. In other terms,

> the purpose of working with supermarkets was not only to create new outlets for local producers, but also to ensure the viability of a logistic tool to also support the development of alternative food networks, and thereby foster the development of a local food system, more sustainable consumption patterns, small-scale holdings and new forms of agri-food governance.
>
> (Bui et al., 2019)

What these contrasting examples illustrate is that, for regime change to occur – to move from mere co-optation to subversion, from the mainstream regime buying time to the mainstream regime being transformed –, two conditions should be present. First, the actors involved should share an understanding of the sustainability challenges to be addressed and of how their individual strategies may contribute to addressing these challenges. This is what we called "systemic ethics" in the study of how local products were gradually promoted in the Belgian retail sector. This, we should emphasize, does not mean that the different rationales of actors, their respective worldviews, or their material interests, should be ignored. Quite to the contrary in fact: such divergences should be fully taken into account, but this should be part of a reflexive process of redefinition of each actor's contribution to the reshaping of the system on which all depend.

We can learn from climate activists trying to communicate about climate change how such systemic ethics can be made to emerge. After many years of testing different ways to speak about climate change, these activists now converge on the main lesson: arguments that may be appealing to some may leave others indifferent, or even meet with outright hostility, and it is therefore necessary to tailor the argument to the particular audience towards which it is directed (Marshall, 2011,

2014; Stoknes, 2015). Such arguments, moreover, shall not be of a rational nature alone; they also should speak to the emotions, to the "values" that the particular group holds, and they should be phrased in ways that can pierce the shield that stands in the path of any message about the need to disrupt establish routines (Lakoff, 2009). The original subtitle of George Lakoff's bestselling book *The Political Mind* was "Why you can't understand 21st-century politics with an 18th-century brain", and it captures well the key message: we can't succeed in convincing people today, he writes in substance, with a view of the mind inherited from Enlightenment theorists, for whom "all you need to do is give people the facts and the figures and they will reach the right conclusion". In such a view,

> You will not have any need to appeal to emotion – indeed, to do so would be wrong! You will not have to speak of values; facts and figures will suffice. You will not have to change people's brains; their reason should be enough. You will not have to frame the facts; they will speak for themselves.
>
> (Lakoff, 2009: 11)

Of course, social innovators seeking to achieve system-wide change are not politicians seeking to convince voters to cast a ballot for them, the chief concern of Lakoff. But the analogies are more important than the differences: both have to reach people's convictions, cutting across a broad spectrum of sensitivities, and focus on empathy as much as on interests. The "systemic ethics" should not only speak to self-interest, nor should it use only rational arguments: it should also strike the right emotional chord.

Second, our research shows that governance arrangements matter. Co-optation occurs when the incumbents of the mainstream regime choose how – at which scale, under which conditions – to incorporate the social innovation they have an interest in adopting. Subversion becomes possible when the social innovators themselves participate in defining how such adoption shall occur. In that sense, economic democracy, which is one important dimension of the social and solidarity economy, should be seen as an essential component of any attempt to steer the mainstream regime towards greater sustainability. Participation is not a luxury, but a necessity. It may require time and resources, but it is the only way to ensure the incorporation of the social innovation shall be transformative. And a new generation of activists is emerging, who are willing to invest in this transformation. We meet them in the following chapter.

References

Alchian, A.A. (1950). Uncertainty, evolution, and economic theory. *Journal of Political Economy*, *58*(3): 211–221.

Allen, P. and Guthman, J. (2006). From "old school" to "farm-to-school": Neoliberalization from the ground up. *Agriculture and Human Values*, *23*(4): 401–415.

Andersson, D. and Nässén J. (2016). The Gothenburg congestion charge scheme: A pre-post analysis of commuting behavior and travel satisfaction. *Journal of Transport Geography*, *52:* 82–89.

Bui, S. (2015). "Pour une approche territoriale des transitions écologiques. Analyse de la transition vers l'agroécologie dans la Biovallée?" (Ph.D. dissertation, Institut des sciences et industries du vivant et de l'environnement, AgroParisTech).

Bui, S., Costa, I., De Schutter, O., Dedeurwaerdere, T., Hudon, M. and Feyereisen, M. (2019). Systemic ethics and inclusive governance: Two key prerequisites for sustainability transitions of agri-food systems. *Agriculture and Human Values*, 1–12, DOI: 10.1007/s10460-019-09917-2.

Centola, D., Becker, J., Brackbill, D. and Baronchelli, A. (2018). Experimental evidence for tipping points in social convention. *Science*, *360*: 1116–1119.

Clark, N. (1985). *The Political Economy of Science and Technology*. Oxford: Basil Blackwell.

Dasgupta, P. and Stiglitz, J. (1988). Potential competition, actual competition, and economic welfare. *European Economic Review*, *32*(2–3): 569–577.

De Haan, H. (2010). "Towards transition theory." (Ph.D. thesis, Erasmus University Rotterdam).

Frank, R., Gilovic, T. and Regan, D.T. (1993). Does studying economics inhibit cooperation? *Journal of Economic Perspectives*, *7*(2): 159–171.

Geels, F.W. (2002). Technological transitions as evolutionary reconfiguration processes: A multi-level perspective and a case- study. *Research Policy*, *31*(8–9): 1257–1274.

Geels, F.W. (2011). The multi-level perspective on sustainability transitions: Responses to seven criticisms. *Environmental Innovations and Societal Transformations*, *1*: 24–40.

Geels, F.W. and Schot, J. (2007). Typology of sociotechnical transition pathways. *Research Policy*, *36*(3): 399–417.

Grin, J. (2010). Understanding transitions from a government perspective. In: Grin, J., Rotmans, J. and Schot, J. (eds.). *Transitions to Sustainable Development: New Directions in the Study of Long-term Transformative Change*: 223–338. London: Routledge.

Guthman, J. (2008). Neoliberalism and the making of food politics in California. *Geoforum*, *39*(3): 1171–1183.

Halpern, D. (2015). *Inside the Nudge Unit. How Small Changes Can Make a Big Difference*. London: WH Allen.

Hege, E. (2016). "Scaling up social innovation for sustainable development? The allocation of roles in community–corporate partnerships for renewable energy projects in the EU." (Master thesis, Sciences Po, Paris School for International Affairs (PSIA)).

Hoogma, R., Kemp, R., Schot, J. and Truffer, B. (2002). *Experimenting for Sustainable Transport: The Approach of Strategic Niche Management.* London: Spon Press.

Jacobsson, S. and Johnson, A. (2000). The diffusion of renewable energy technology: An analytical framework and key issues for research. *Energy Policy, 28*(9): 625–640.

Kahneman, D. (2011). *Thinking, Fast and Slow.* New York: Farrar, Straus & Giroux.

Kemp, R., Rotmans, J. and Loorbach, D. (2007). Assessing the Dutch energy transition policy: How does it deal with dilemmas of managing transitions? *Journal of Environmental Policy & Planning, 9*(3–4): 315–331.

Klein, N. (2007). *The Shock Doctrine: The Rise of Disaster Capitalism.* New York: Macmillan.

Kuran, T. (1995). *Private Truths, Public Lies: The Social Consequences of Preference Falsification.* Harvard: Harvard University Press.

Lakoff, G. (2009). *The Political Mind: A Cognitive Scientist's Guide to Your Brain and Its Politics.* London: Penguin Books.

Marshall, G. (2011). *How to Engage Your Community and Communicate about Climate Change.* Climate Outreach Information Network. Retreived online: https://climateoutreach.org

Marshall, G. (2014). *Don't Even Think About It: Why Our Brains Are Wired to Ignore Climate Change.* London: Bloomsbury.

McCarthy, M. (2010). *The Ecology of Innovation.* London: RSA.

McClintock, N. (2014). Radical, reformist, and garden-variety neoliberal: Coming to terms with urban agriculture's contradictions. *Local Environment, 19*(2): 147–171.

McKibben, B. (2007). *Deep Economy: The Wealth of Communities and the Durable Future.* New York: Henry Holt & Co.

Mert-Cakal, T. and Miele, M. (2020). 'Workable utopias' for social change through inclusion and empowerment? Community supported agriculture (CSA) in Wales as social innovation. *Agriculture and Human Values, 37*: 1241–1260.

NESTA. (2009). *People-Powered Responses to Climate Change: Mapping Community-Led Proposals to NESTA's Big Green Challenge.* London: NESTA.

Papargyropoulou, E., Lozano, R., Steinberger, J.K., Wright, N. and en Ujang, Z.B. (2014). The food waste hierarchy as a framework for the management of food surplus and food waste. *Journal of Cleaner Production, 76*: 106–115.

Poteete, A.R., Janssen, M.A. and Ostrom, E. (2010). *Working Together: Collective Action, the Commons, and Multiple Methods in Practice.* Princeton, NJ: Princeton University Press.

Raworth, K. (2013). *Doughnut Economics: Seven Ways to Think Like a 21st-Century Economist.* London: Cornerstone.

Rip, A. and Kemp, R. (1998). Technological change. *Human Choice and Climate Change, 2*(2): 327–399.

Rotmans, J. and Loorbach, D. (2010). Towards a better understanding of transitions and their governance. A systemic and reflexive approach. In: Grin, J., Rotmans, J. and Schot, J. (eds.). *Transitions to Sustainable Development: New Directions in the Study of Long Term Transformative Change*: 105–222. Abingdon-on-Thames: Routledge.

Roza, L., Stubbe, W. and Meijs, L. (2014). Why and how nonprofit organisations, companies and intermediaries can use Corporate Community Involvement to strengthen society. Research findings Rotterdam School of Management, Erasmus University Rotterdam.

Ryan, R. and Deci, E. (2000). Self-determination theory and the facilitation of intrinsic motivation, social development, and well-being. *American Psychologist, 55*(1): 68–78.

Seitanidi, M. and Ryan, A. (2012). A critical review of forms of corporate community involvement: From philanthropy to partnerships. *International Journal of Nonprofit and Voluntary Sector Marketing, 12*(3): 247–266.

Servan-Schreiber, D. (2018). *Super collectif. La nouvelle puissance de nos intelligences.* Paris: Fayard.

Seyfang, G. and Haxeltine, A. (2012). Growing grassroots innovations: Exploring the role of community-based initiatives in governing sustainable energy transitions. *Environment and Planning C: Government and Policy, 30*(3): 381–400.

Seyfang, G., Hielscher, S., Hargreaves, T., Martiskainen, M. and Smith, A. (2014). A grassroots sustainable energy niche? Reflections on community energy in the UK. *Environmental Innovation and Societal Transitions, 13*: 21–44.

Seyfang, G. and Smith, A. (2007). Grassroots innovations for sustainable development: Towards a new research and policy agenda. *Environmental Politics, 16*(4): 584–603.

Shove, E. (2003). *Comfort, Cleanliness and Convenience: The Social Organisation of Normality.* Oxford: Berg.

Slocock, C., Harker, D. and Hayes, R. (2015). *Whose Society? The Final Big Society Audit* (London, Civil Exchange). Retreived online: https://www.civilexchange.org

Stiglitz, J.E. (1987). Technological change, sunk costs, and competition. *Brookings Papers on Economic Activity, 3*: 883–947.

Stoknes, P.E. (2015). *What We Think about When We Try Not to Think about Global Warming.* Chelsea: Chelsea Green Publ.

Sunstein, C.R. (1996). Social norms and social roles. *Columbia Law Review, 96*: 903–968.

Thaler, R. (2015). *Misbehaving: The Making of Behavioural Economics.* London: Penguin Books.

Tversky, A. and Kahneman, R. (1991). Loss aversion in riskless choice: A reference-dependent model. *Quarterly Journal of Economics, 106*: 1039–1061.

4 The new activism

Just like there are different understandings of how the regime can be made to change, there are different categories of activists seeking to bring about such change: Geels (2011), for instance, has tried to relate transformative possibilities to different profiles of activists working to change the system (as mapped in Dahle, 2007). We are interested here, however, in one particular branch of activism. We are interested in those who do things, because they believe in their ability to improve their environment, without wanting to wait for solutions to come from outside or from above: these are the activists who nurture community gardens, establish energy cooperatives, or create alternative community currencies.

This particular brand of activism is the product of disappointment with technocratic solutions. As societies have grown more complex and problems more intractable, and as the role of the State in the economy has continuously expanded – whether to deliver welfare entitlements or to introduce the set of regulations, monitoring devices, and market-based mechanisms typical of the recent retreat of the welfare State –, governments have sought to rely not only on large bureaucracies but also on experts, whose specialized knowledge is seen as a promise of successful public policy. This tendency accompanied the establishment of the modern State (Weber, 1978). It is now showing its limits. As a counter-weight to this expert knowledge, the lay knowledge of social actors is emerging as an essential source of innovation; and in opposition to technocratic solutions, in which political action is relegated to an essentially legitimizing function, a new demand for democratic empowerment is emerging (Graeber, 2013; Van Reybrouck, 2014; Boucher, 2017). The crisis of democracy, moreover, goes beyond the crisis of a particular model of democratic representation in which the citizen casts a vote every four or five years, electing representatives who then have a mandate to act in the name of the population –

DOI: 10.4324/9781003223542-4

deciding for all and thinking for them, rather than co-constructing with them. The crisis runs deeper: what emerges is not just a gap between the "governing elites" and the "people", but a new scepticism towards the political system itself, whose ability to effectuate social transformation is now openly put in doubt. Why should we aim at recapturing the State, if the State has become a paper tiger, unable to change the trajectory of societies?

The new activism expressed in community-led social innovations is not directed against any political camp in particular. It is not even directed against politics as such. It is, in that sense, neither reformist (proposing an alternative political program) nor revolutionary (proposing to wither existing institutions and replace them with other institutions). Rather, to the new activists, politics belong to a different world. Theirs is a world of action, not of discourse. Their priority is to do things, not to call upon others to have things done. Governments in their view are at best temporary allies for the construction of an initiative (for they can provide grants, after all, or lend their technical expertise); at worst, they are seen as obstructing the flow of the initiatives that are emerging from below. To many of them, it is not that some politicians perform better than others, or have more attractive programs: it is that they have lost touch with what happens at the local level, and that politics, as a way to transform society, has become close to irrelevant.

There is a generational aspect to this crisis of politics. When Albert Hirschman sought to study how discontent could express itself in the 1960s, he presented his memorable 'exit, voice, and loyalty' scheme, which essentially meant this: unless the person dissatisfied with a product or a service decided to remain loyal to the producer or to the provider, she had a choice either to 'exit' (typically, to switch to another brand) or to 'voice' her concern (signalling her discontent to the firm, which could lead the firm to improve its performance) (Hirschman, 1970). Whereas economists typically have focused on the 'exit' reaction to the decline in product quality ('consumer sovereignty' resides essentially in the ability of the individual consumer to 'opt out' of a brand and to turn to a competing brand, which is possible except in situations of monopoly), political scientists have generally paid greater attention to how people may express their 'voice'. The original contribution of Hirschman was to bring together both means of expressing preferences – 'revealed', in the economist's perspective, by how people act as consumers, and 'voiced', in the perspective of the political scientist, who imagined that dissatisfied consumers might act, not as market participants only, but as citizens do: by protesting.

Hirschman had a rather extensive understanding of how, in this scheme, 'voice' could be expressed: he defined 'voice' as

> any attempt at all to change, rather than to escape from, an objectionable state of affairs, whether through individual or collective petition to the management directly in charge, through appeal to higher authority with the intention of forcing a change in management, or through various types of actions and protests, including those that are meant to mobilize public opinion.
>
> (Hirschman, 1970: 30)

It is however remarkable that these various manifestations of 'voice' remain within the boundaries of the consumer society. In this framework, a consumer disappointed with apples may turn to oranges ("exit"), and a driver of a Ford disappointed with his car may write to Ford's management ("voice"). But Hirschman did not consider that disappointment could also lead the consumer to 'exit' in a more radical way – by growing one's own orchard, for example, by setting up a car-sharing scheme with neighbours, or by dispensing with a car altogether. Nor, initially, did he take into account that consumer dissatisfaction might lead him to genuinely political action: comparing different political programs, in order to identify which referred to improving food quality or car safety, and voting.

When, ten years after *Exit, Voice, and Loyalty*, Hirschman returned to the issue, he confessed at least to this last limitation of his initial model:

> If important private consumption experiences that had been particularly looked forward to as presumed dispensers of 'happiness' leave behind them a trail of disappointment and frustration and if, at the same time, a wholly different 'pursuit of happiness', say, political action, is available to the disappointed consumer, is it likely that this pursuit will be taken up at some favorable occasion?
>
> (Hirschman, 1982: 63)

The answer of Hirschman to this question, in the form of an implicit self-critique, was affirmative: at least if "we deal with consumers who are also conscious of being citizens", we can plausibly expect that some will turn to public action, that is, to politics. In the book he published in 1982, aptly titled *Shifting Involvements: Private Interest and Public Action*, he examined in that spirit under which conditions one might move from an exclusive focus on the private and on consumption to involvement in public action – that is, from acting as a consumer/ buyer, albeit a potentially dissatisfied one that voices his concerns or changes his purchasing practices, to act as a citizen/voter. That was an important contribution at the time, not least because it contrasted with the general scepticism towards collective action nourished by studies such as Mancur Olson's *Logic of Collective Action* (published in 1965). Taking as departure point a characteristically economicist understanding of human motivations, premised on the idea of the rational and utility-maximizing agent, Olson seemed to deny even the very possibility of people investing in collective action when they could more comfortably behave as free riders benefiting from the efforts of others. Hirschman instead sought to demonstrate why, despite the apparent futility – or irrationality – of political action, this was a form of action people might still engage in.

Even thus revised and expanded, however, the scheme of Hirschman remained incomplete. At the time of his writing – the 1970s –, political activism was reaching unprecedented high levels, fuelled in the United States by the struggle for civil rights and the mobilization against the Vietnam War (both of which had really started in the 1960s). A contemporary Hirschman would be confronted with a rather different picture, however.

The activism of the 1960s and 1970s, it could be argued, led to two quite different ramifications in the following two decades. First, starting in the 1970s, there emerged a radical critique of the consumer society. Rachel Carson published *Silent Spring* in 1962, starting the modern environmentalist movement in the United States. Ten years later, the report *The Limits to Growth*, commissioned in 1972 by the Club of Rome to MIT researchers led by Dennis Meadows, drew the attention of public opinion to the unsustainable nature of our consumption patterns. Economists such as John K. Galbraith, in *The Affluent Society* (1958), Tibor Scitovsky, in *The Joyless Economy* (1976), or Fred Hirsch, in *Social Limits to Growth* (1976), noted the addictive nature of consumption, warning against the manufacturing of desires by the advertising industry and by social comparison. These authors also remarked that with the growth of the consumer society, many goods that originally might have served a "signalling" function within the community, allowing their owner to stand out in comparison to his peers, had become so widely affordable and used that they could only be a source of disappointment to the consumer: André Gorz's study on the "ideology of the car" provides a remarkable illustration of this critique (Gorz, 1975). All this led to a widely shared discontent with the post-World War II growth model, which occasionally moves beyond rhetorics: in the 1970s, some groups actually did seek to invent alternative lifestyles, based on a norm of sufficiency rather than of endless accumulation, and putting quality of life above gains in material consumption.

In contrast, however, the 1980s and 1990s were dominated by the spread of individualism and consumerism, and by what Castoriadis called "privatization" – the retreat of the individual to the private sphere, his or her removal from political action, which is both a cause and a consequence of the separation between the governing and the governed (Castoriadis, 1996: 25 and 77–79). The erosion of "social capital", discussed above, is one consequence of this trend. The most direct explanation for this development was the start of the economic crisis in 1973–1974. One of the effects of the crisis was to create a sudden panic, particularly since it unfolded at a time when access to higher-level education had been significantly democratized (for figures concerning the growth of university education in Western Europe during the period 1950–1970, see Judt, 2005: 392–394): for the first time since the world wars, the generation that came to maturity during those years were not certain that they would fare better than their parents, and they were not certain even to be able to find a job corresponding to their qualifications. Another explanation for this retreat, however, and for the massive growth of individualism during this period, may have been the spread of a neoliberal ethos, in which material success was praised as the mark of the successful individual's "merit" – markets, after all, by definition would have sanctioned any unwise choice he or she might have made. The fall of the Berlin Wall in 1989, finally, led to a sense of inevitability of the then present order of things: politics were discounted as futile, in the absence of real alternatives to the joint rule of the market economy and Western-style democracy based on elections. Indeed, the social democratic parties themselves either had shifted their attention to cultural issues and to the protection of minorities' rights (Schiller, 2015), or they had espoused an agenda premised on the reform of the welfare State to make it leaner and more efficient. In their quest to reduce "dependency on handouts" and to ensure a shift from "welfare" to "workfare", however, they were gradually eroding the boundaries that separated them from their right-wing adversaries, and many of their traditional supporters turned away in disenchantment (for influential contributions preparing or theorizing this transformation of social democracy, see Giddens, 1994, 1998 and 2000; for a study of the impacts on the organization of the welfare State, see Hemerijck, 2013 and De Schutter, 2015).

Each generation defines itself, in part, by what previous generations have achieved, and by the legacy – both of ideas and of institutions – that they have transmitted. Subjects have histories. And what lessons can the current generation draw from the experiences of their parents and grandparents? Two lessons in particular: first, despite all the warnings from scientists, that started in the late 1950s already, our societies have remained on an unsustainable course; second, attempts to change the direction of progress by political action – by demonstrating on the streets, by joining political parties, or by union action – have proven futile, despite all the rhetorical pledges to move to more sustainable development pathways and some marginal progress on the ground. The student revolts of the late 1960s were typically directed against the consumer society and the idea that the emancipation and flourishing of the individual could result from increases in the possibilities of material consumption. Whether, in some perverse betrayal of their emancipatory potential, such libertarian impulses might have paved the way for the growth of the individualistic, or even narcissistic, ethos of the 1980s, has become a subject of controversy (Boltanski and Chiapello, 1999). But what at least cannot be denied is that the hopes of the 1960s and 1970s have been disappointed.

This forms the background of the current forms of civic engagement. The rise of the "do-it-yourself democracy", as well as of community-led social innovations that have their source in citizens' initiatives at the grassroots level, is in part the result of the disenchantment of this generation. Classic forms of public action, the millennials intuitively feel, have failed us. There is a need for innovative ways of changing patterns of production and consumption if we want to have a chance, even minimal, to slow down before we reach the cliff. The decision tree, therefore, now looks very different (see Figure 4.1).

Instead of a simple "exit, voice or loyalty" framework, we have various forms of "exit" to express dissatisfaction with a particular product or service: such "exit" may take the form either of opting for another (competing) product or service, or of creating alternatives and "opting out" of the mainstream market altogether. Similarly, "voice" may be exercised by protesting against the company concerned, as in Hirschman's initial scheme, but also by shifting to political action, whether by exercising one's right to vote or joining a political party, or by creating alternative deliberative fora to expand the scope of democratic deliberation. This latter route is illustrated by the establishment of food policy councils, initially in Northern America but now increasingly in Europe, as deliberative fora where actors of the food

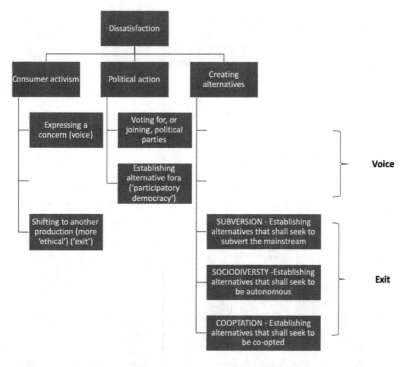

Figure 4.1 Different reactions to the dissatisfaction with the status quo. Figure by the authors.

system co-construct proposals to improve the food system (Fox, 2010; Moragues-Faus et al., 2013).

These different options are not necessarily mutually exclusive. An individual may for instance, at any point in time, at the same time opt for products on the supermarket shelves that comply with certain requirements linked to sustainability (for example, as signalled by labelling schemes); join a CSA scheme through which he will have direct access to a local producer; and take part in deliberations, within a local council, in which the reform of the local food system shall be debated. These different options do relate to one another, however: the more a certain option shall be difficult or costly to exercise, the more the other options shall be seen as attractive. (For instance, if there is no affordable alternative to industrially processed foods in the vicinity, making the "exit" to different food products difficult, the conscious eater may decide to join forces with neighbours to launch a

CSA scheme, or to establish a food policy council with a view to improving the food supply.)

The creation of alternatives itself, the third option presented in the figure above, may take different forms, depending both on the intention of animating the initiators and on the relationship that the alternative shall gradually develop with the mainstream system. A first form corresponds to the scenario (#2) of socio-diversity referred to above: an alternative is established, that cherishes its autonomy above all, and that remains at arms' length from any involvement with either mainstream market actors or with political actors. A second form corresponds to the scenario (#3) of co-optation: the alternative grows to finally morph into a form of entrepreneurship, that the mainstream regime shall easily absorb. A third form finally corresponds to the scenario (#4) of subversion: the alternative becomes a source of inspiration to question the established routines within the mainstream regime.

"Exit" and "Voice" should therefore not be seen as the two branches of an alternative. They are, rather, complementary, and for the individual actor, the latter may in fact follow the former. Consider for instance the Open Works project in South London, which seems to encourage the participation of residents in peer-to-peer initiatives with free participation and low thresholds in time, skills, and budget, enabling in principle anyone to join. The aim of the project is to encourage community participation in productive activities. Interviews conducted with 30 participants in the project in 2014–2015 confirmed, however, that such involvement in community activities led them gradually to develop an increased interest in public life and in political activism: by taking part in a community project in their neighbourhood, these participants acquired new skills; they gained confidence in their ability to achieve things; their levels of trust in others increased, and so did their willingness to join in further collective actions (Detroux, 2016). In the terms of our typology, what initially looked like an initiative, Open Works, seeking to create "sociodiversity", might easily develop in a breeding ground for politically motivated activists, prepared to take part in the institutional life of their community.

Other such connections between "Exit" and "Voice" and between consumer activism, political action and the creation of alternatives, may be identified. In particular, where the scenario (#3) of co-optation is the preferred one, the design of the alternative shall quite naturally seek to fit the exigencies of the mainstream regime, which in its dominant form is geared towards profit-making: it shall be formatted with a view to facilitate such co-optation, in particular by facilitating the

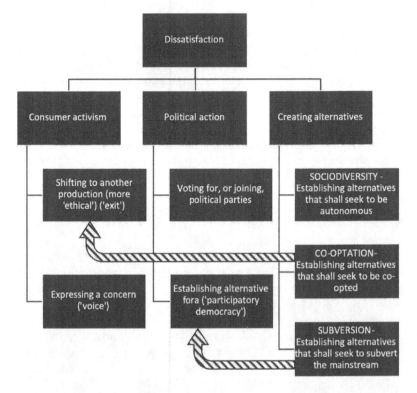

Figure 4.2 How different reactions to the dissatisfaction with the status quo relate to one another. Figure by the authors.

role of critical consumers. Similarly, the scenario (#4) of subversion shall generally imply working with the public authorities, and possibly participating in public decision-making, so as to ensure that the policy and regulatory environment shall be hospitable to the gradual expansion, or "scaling out", of the alternative: the establishment of participatory forms of democracy shall be seen as attractive because it allows for such a scenario to develop. Such connections can be illustrated graphically (see Figure 4.2).

What emerges is a complex picture of how various forms of involvement in societal change interact. These forms are of course different and certain trade-offs may exist: though not mutually exclusive, they can be perceived therefore as competing against one another. Yet they are in fact complementary, and they shall in most cases succeed one another, or supplement each other, in the life course of any single individual.

References

Boltanski, L. and Chiapello, E. (1999). *Le nouvel esprit du capitalisme.* Paris: Gallimard.

Boucher, S. (2017). Petit manuel de créativité politique. Comment libérer l'audace collective. Paris: Editions du Félin.

Castoriadis, C. (1996). *La montée de l'insignifiance. Les carrefours du labyrinthe (Tome 4).* Paris: Le Seuil.

Dahle, K. (2007). When do transformative initiatives really transform? A typology of different paths for transition to a sustainable society. *Futures, 39*: 487–504.

De Schutter, O. (2015) Welfare state reform and social rights. *Netherlands Quarterly of Human Rights, 33*(2): 123–162.

Detroux, A. (2016). "The productive community: Can ecosystems of community participation lead to a culture of political engagement?" (Unpublished dissertation, MSc in Public Policy and Administration, London School of Economics and Political Science).

Fox, C. (2010). Food Policy Councils. Innovations in Democratic Governance for A Sustainable and Equitable Food System. UCLA Planning Department. Retrieved online: https://goodfoodlosangeles.files.wordpress.com/2011/01/pc_final_dist-5-indd.pdf

Galbraith, J.K. (1958). *The Affluent Society.* New York: Houghton Mifflin Co.

Geels, F.W. (2011). The multi-level perspective on sustainability transitions: Responses to seven criticisms. *Environmental Innovations and Societal Transformations, 1*: 24–40.

Giddens, A. (1994). *Beyond Left and Right: The Future of Radical Politics.* Cambridge: Polity Press.

Giddens, A. (1998). *The Third Way: The Renewal of Social Democracy.* Cambridge: Polity Press.

Giddens, A. (2000). *The Third Way and Its Critics.* Cambridge: Polity Press.

Gorz, A. (1975). *Ecologie et politique.* Paris: Galilée.

Graeber, D. (2013). *The Democracy Project: A History. A Crisis. A Moment.* London: Allen Lane.

Hemerijck, A. (2013). *Changing Welfare States.* Oxford: Oxford University Press.

Hirsch, F. (1976). *Social Limits to Growth.* Cambridge, MA: Harvard University Press.

Hirschman, A.O. (1970). *Exit, Voice and Loyalty: Responses to Decline in Firms, Organizations and States.* Cambridge, MA: Harvard University Press.

Hirschman, A.O. (1982). *Shifting Involvements: Private Interest and Public Action.* Princeton, NJ and Oxford: Princeton University Press.

Judt, T. (2005). *Postwar: A History of Europe since 1945.* New York: The Penguin Press.

Moragues, A., Morgan, K., Moschitz, H., Neimane, I., Nilsson, H., Pinto, M., Rohracher,H., Ruiz, R., Thuswald, M., Tisenkopfs, T. and Halliday, J. (2013).

68   *The new activism*

Urban Food Strategies: The Rough Guide to Sustainable Food Systems. Retrieved online: http://www.fao.org/urban-food-actions/resources/resources-detail/en/c/1142480/

Schiller, R. (2015) *Forging Rivals: Race, Class, Law, and the Collapse of Postwar Liberalism*. Cambridge, MA: Cambridge University Press.

Scitovsky, T. (1976). *The Joyless Economy: The Psychology of Human Satisfaction*. Oxford: Oxford University Press. (2nd ed. 1992).

Van Reybrouck, D. (2014). *Contre les élections*. Arles: Actes Sud.

Weber, M. (1978). *Economy and Society*. Berkeley: University of California Press.

5 Enabling societal transformation without the myths

The new brand of activism that emerged with this millennium is one that seeks to do things, not to call upon others to have things done. The role of social innovations is therefore more crucial than ever. For the transition to sustainable societies, many hopes are placed in technological innovations: to a large extent, the promise of "green growth" is that cleaner technologies shall allow to shift to more sustainable modes of production and consumption, and thus to reduce the ecological impacts of growth. This, we are told, should allow all populations to adopt the lifestyles of the most affluent nations, without crossing the thresholds that endanger the viability of the planet and the future of human civilization.

It is a promise we would like to be able to believe. Yet, we argued above that, however crucial it is to accelerate the dissemination of clean, resource-efficient technologies, it would be wrong to believe that they are sufficient to move us out of the ecological and social impasse. Technological progress without lifestyle changes simply cannot deliver the kind of transformation we need: while some areas of transformation are indeed technology-dependent such as in the field of energy production, in most areas, such as in the fields of mobility, food, housing and amongst others, transformation is based on indispensable lifestyle and behavioural changes. Moreover, under certain conditions, as we have seen, resource-efficient technologies may even lead to increased consumption, an effect known as the "rebound effect". New technologies, moreover, are often highly resource-intensive, to such an extent that this may counterbalance any improvement in eco-efficiency. The example of the Internet is telling: in spite of the rhetoric of "de-materialization", new digital technologies push for ever more intensive use of data centres that are still powered by fossil energy sources, amongst others by ever more sophisticated consumer technologies for using large photos, banner, pop-ups and cloud-based

DOI: 10.4324/9781003223542-5

programmes on the Internet. In addition, the Internet's role in decreasing resource use through collaboration in areas such as mobility or housing has remained ambiguous at best. In most cities major sharing economy companies such as Uber or Airbnb have resulted in increased car use, in the growth of city trips (made more affordable thanks to a platform such as Airbnb), or even in the building of *ad hoc* tourism infrastructure.

In contrast, the lifestyle changes required in such essential fields of human activity as mobility, housing, or food are often prepared by the social innovations developed by people in poverty. Produce more with fewer resources; save, and avoid waste; cherish diversity as a source of resilience; rely on sharing and solidarity networks as the ultimate insurance policy against economic downturns and natural disasters: these are some of the lessons they teach, and these are the lessons we must learn from them. While the shift to low-carbon lifestyles might lead to sacrificing some potential improvement in well-being in some areas (including some improvements that could be brought about by new technologies), such losses are largely compensated by well-being improvements in other areas such as an increase in social capital, quality of work, or family relationships (Larsson and Bolin, 2014).

Unlike technological innovations, social innovations for lifestyle changes cannot be fenced by intellectual property rights, and they are not handed over from scientists and engineers working in large firms to users. Instead, they are democratic. They rely on large-scale collaboration of all actors involved in society-wide transformations. They are shared in open access. They are grown organically and bottom-up. They do not lead to centralization, but to decentralization. They do not lead to the dissemination of uniform solutions, demanding from people that they adapt to technologies that are imposed on them in the name of "progress". Instead, social innovations promote and value diversity. They result from the search by local communities of the solutions that are best suited to the particular contexts in which they live. They do not disempower, and they do not result in new dependencies: they are empowering and promote autonomy and self-determination.

Therefore, clean and resource-efficient technologies are not a substitute for the large-scale, collaborative, and system-wide lifestyle changes in mobility, housing, food, recycling, etc. Social innovations in these fields have a crucial role to play in realizing the kind of transformative change needed to overcome the current impasse (Stamm et al., 2009). In this context, the idea that we need to fundamentally change research, technology, and innovation policy has continuously gained support in the debates about sustainable development. It has achieved a strong momentum in the European debate on Grand Challenges (Kuhlmann and Rip, 2014). To realize long-term transformative change, according to this emerging consensus, more will be needed than technological product or process innovation at the level of the firm. Rather, comprehensive system innovations should be implemented, which can generate novel configurations of actors, institutions, and practices that bring about new modes of operations of entire sectors or systems of production and consumption (Weber and Rohracher, 2012: 1037).

The "do-it-yourself" democracy practiced by the new activists can be nurtured. This chapter makes six concrete proposals that, we believe, could support the emergence of citizens-led social innovations. They range from the organization of research to the support of the social and solidarity economy and from the promotion of sustainable finance to the shift in public action from the imposition of mandates to the encouragement of local experimentation. The list is certainly incomplete, and even the content of the proposals listed remains tentative. But we are firmly convinced that, contrary to the cliché of citizens-led social innovations that emerge spontaneously, the environment matters. We may create a fertile breeding ground, or not. We cannot, by definition, force innovation: it is the very characteristic of true innovation that it cannot be anticipated, and thus it cannot be "planned". But, by creating the right breeding ground, we can increase our chances of reaping the benefits from the imagination of communities.

Proposal #1: Changing the innovation pathways: from rent-seeking technologies to transdisciplinary research

Sustainability scientists acknowledge that, to implement long-term transformations of entire socio-technological systems, we need to move from interdisciplinary approaches to transdisciplinary collaborations (OECD, 2020). Such alliances bring together academic and non-academic expertise from social actors and citizens involved in transformative social change. In particular, solving sustainability problems involves decisions on values that require civic participation and the building of broad social legitimacy. Reviewing over a decade of experience with transdisciplinary research, Jahn et al. (2012) have defined transdisciplinarity as a "critical and self-reflexive research approach that relates societal with scientific problems; it produces new knowledge by integrating different scientific and extra-scientific insights; its aim is to contribute to both societal and scientific progress". Which transition pathways to sustainable societies we should explore should be the outcome of such co-construction, not the result of top-down impositions. As pointed out by Grin et al. (2010: 107),

> our transdisciplinary approach [to transitions] does not only rely on the input of scientific knowledge and expertise, but also on participatory research. Because transition research also seeks to contribute to a more sustainable society, action research plays a prominent role as well. The exchange of knowledge between scientists and societal actors to which our approach gives rise does not follow a linear path but rather entails a societal process of co-production between the parties involved.

Transdisciplinary research aims to integrate knowledge from various scientific and societal bodies of knowledge, ensuring an adequate hybridization between "expert" and "lay" knowledge, or between the expertise of scientists and that of social actors. It is based on the idea that practitioners are better positioned to identify solutions that work in the particular context in which they operate. Their involvement in research can thus improve both the legitimacy and the relevance of the findings. This is especially important for research that aims at identifying the levers that can bring about lifestyle changes, since such changes require an understanding of the motivations of the actors involved, as well as of the constraints they face (Hirsch Hadorn, 2008; Lang et al., 2012).

It is therefore particularly important where the objective is strong sustainability, which rejects the substitution of man-made capital (whether physical or financial) to natural capital, and that therefore resists the monetization of nature and ecosystem services.

The practice of transdisciplinary research for sustainability relies on a permanent interaction between research and social innovations, in which research is the product of a co-construction between academic experts and social practitioners, and in which social innovations gradually improve in the light of any shortcomings research has helped to highlight, in what may be described as an iterative learning process (Figure 5.1).

A team of researchers conducted a systematic comparative analysis of 20 large-scale transdisciplinary research projects in Europe (Herrero et al., 2018; and see Table 5.1). The analysis showed that by a combination of co-construction methods that explicitly address normative agendas and orientations, and appropriate governance of the collaborative process amongst actors and scientists, transdisciplinary research projects can effectively generate social learning on social and ecological transition. Social learning has proven to be truly

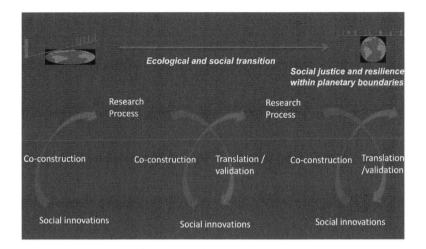

Figure 5.1 Interaction process between knowledge generated within social innovations and scientific research on social and ecological transition. Figure by the authors.

transformational when it leads to reframing the problem to be solved (visible through a change in representations of the system, of the social norms or the power structures) or in challenging the objectives and values that guide the definition of the research question and methodology.

The comparative study identified three major factors promoting social learning in such transdisciplinary research projects:

1   *Openness of the co-construction of the research question*: the more the methodology allowed affected actors to get involved in the framing of the research question, of the method and of the objectives as well as in the selection of stakeholders, the more the process generated social learning;
2   *Clarification of the normative background*: the more the goals behind the research process were openly discussed and the broader the range of techniques have been used to exchange about normative agendas of the concerned actors, the more the process was able to build trust and reciprocal understanding for social learning;
3   *Balancing distribution of power (resources/powerful actors)*: when governance processes were put into place to balance power games and to compensate for resource limitations, researchers and practitioners were able to organize more lasting social learning processes.

74   *Enabling societal transformation*

Table 5.1 Examples of research partnerships with societal actors that were successful in generating social learning

Project name and duration	Researchers partnered with	Country
1 Transition toolbox, four years	agro-stakeholders and regional authorities to co-create a transition toolbox	France
2 Forestry conflicts, one year	inhabitants and influent stakeholders to discuss forest management and access to resources through a role-playing game	Thailand
3 Hens farming, five years	organic farmer cooperative to discuss various forms of hens farming through the creation of an Internet site	Germany
4 Cultural landscape, five years	a biosphere reserve and the tourist sector to develop measures preserving the cultural landscape in the face of climate change	Germany
5 Merging knowledge, one, five years	NGO, people with life experience in poverty (PLEP), and social workers to co-produce local and European recommendations to improve the situation of PLEP and practitioners	Poland
6 Sustainable island, four years	environmental NGOs, local authorities, local cooperatives, farmers, lawyers, ministries, and other stakeholders to accompany the sustainable development of an island	Greece
7 Energy targets, one year	citizens, political actors, private companies, and environmental NGOs to co-produce recommendations to make the territory "zero-net energy"	Belgium
8 Detecting pollution, two years	various users of a marine environment to co-plan a strategy to detect pollution in the gulf area	France

Source: The authors, adapted from Herrero et al. (2018) (containing detailed references and additional information on the cases).

The "Sustainable Island" project, for instance – case 6 in Table 5.1–, scores very high on social learning. The coding scale gives the highest score to projects that challenge the understanding of the problem situation and the social values, and lead to an effective collaboration between the scientific expertise, the expertise of the practitioners, and the knowledge outcomes of local social experimentations. In the "Sustainable Island" project, the challenges facing this small Greek island of Samothraki, home to around 2,800 permanent residents, were initially analysed by the mainstream actors through a conventional economic lens, revolving around developing specialized economic niches on the island that provide some competitive advantage in the global economy. Such growth, however, is driven primarily by external pressures from the mainland and reinforces the perceived need for external support to the islands' economic growth. The collaborative dialogues held between scientists and practitioners led to a major reframing of the challenges facing the island in relation to long-term sustainability. Indeed, the transdisciplinary research perspective focused on the understanding of the biophysical attributes and institutional specificities of insularity, as well as insular identity. From this different starting point, researchers and social actors collectively fleshed out an alternative vision of sustaining the local population, in both economic and non-economic dimensions, while maintaining its natural and cultural heritage. The result of this reframing also connected the search for sustainability solutions to the practical real-life problems of the participating inhabitants. For instance, the project developed a smartphone application for livestock management, which convinced farmers that having fewer animals may be better for the land and reduce work, without necessarily reducing profit margins. Moreover, the process led to the creation by the inhabitants of a new association dedicated to implementing the shared vision resulting from the project.

Case 8 of Table 5.1 ("detecting pollution") also received a very high score on social learning. In this project, the research work on marine pollution led to considering more long-term sustainable development issues in the Gulf of Fos-sur-Mer (France) and to an increased involvement of citizen scientists in collecting data and samples on these issues. Moreover, the involved citizens discussed the results of the analysis of pollution samples with the scientists with a view to jointly evaluating the practical implications and programming of further work.

As can be seen from this short overview, transdisciplinary research integrates the concern with technological and economic solutions within a broader approach to the life-world values that really matter to the concerned actors and that builds capacity allowing the less resourceful actors to be fully involved. Indeed, research and innovation will only be effective for promoting re-orienting entire innovation systems towards improved sustainability if such innovation is able to consider multiple societal values to combine different framings of the problem in a way that is socially inclusive. Alongside some successes, many cases illustrate a failure to bridge the science-society gap in sustainability research when the social actors were not involved, or were only poorly involved, in the knowledge gathering and the building of the research design. In particular, the technological innovation systems approach discussed above, which focuses on "green growth" through clean technologies, but without lifestyle changes, typically fails to address the social acceptability of new technologies and the social learning on their effective use for more sustainable behaviour; it also does not protect from the stated risk of various "rebound effects" associated with the improved efficiency of green technologies. As a result, the approach fails to support a broad social transition to sustainable production and consumption even if it increases our understanding of firm-level technological innovations for sustainability. In contrast, transition theory scholars underline the positive role of participatory and collaborative methods for supporting sustainability transitions, as illustrated through the transdisciplinary modes of research (Hirsch Hadorn, 2008).

Proposal #2: Changing capitalism: from the extractive economy to the social and solidarity economy

We saw earlier that citizens-led social innovations developed within "innovation niches" were often faced with a dilemma, between the risk of co-optation by the mainstream regime and its dominant, profit-driven actors; and the opposite risk of marginalization, when the innovation remains segregated in a protected space. The social and solidarity economy provides a way out of the dilemma. Seyfang and Smith emphasize this point, noting that there is a form of congruence between grassroots innovations and the social economy in two respects, which they call respectively social and ideological: the social economy, they note, "provides flexible, localized services in situations where the market cannot", and it is therefore more inclusive, catering to needs (including both social and environmental) and not simply bowing to demand; moreover, grassroots innovations and the social economy share a common "ideological commitment to alternative ways of doing things", which "run counter to the hegemony of the regime" (Seyfang and Smith, 2007: 591–592).

Scholars of socio-ecological transition have shown a growing interest in the contributions of social enterprises to sustainable development (Johanisova et al., 2013). In this context, they consider social enterprises not simply as a tool to address social problems generated by market imperfections, but also as an organizational model that supports social innovations for transition to more sustainable consumption and production practices. More specifically, by accessing a series of non-market resources (such as affordable small loans, lower-than-market rent for premises, and various sharing arrangements for the use of resources), social enterprises can provide an effective survival strategy for transition initiatives, which would otherwise not be able to survive in increasingly competitive markets focused on satisfying the short term expectations of shareholders.

Social enterprises are not to be confused with associations of the voluntary, non-profit sector. In contrast to such associations, social enterprises are involved in market activities, even though they may rely on a mix of paid and voluntary labour. They are specific, however, since they give priority in their market-oriented activities to their societal mission, which can be related to social, cultural, and/ or environmental purposes (Chell, 2007). The primacy of the social aim is generally reflected in constraints on the distribution of profits (Lambert et al., 2019). These constraints are a means to prevent pure profit-maximizing behaviours (Defourny and Nyssens, 2010; Lambert et al., 2019). Such constraints range from a total prohibition of any distribution of profits to other, more flexible limitations. The total non-profit constraint is usually defined by a non-distribution constraint of profits to members, investors, managers, or other types of stakeholders. In the case of a limited distribution constraint, members receive some compensation within a clearly legally specified framework, as illustrated by several new legal forms for social enterprises in European countries (Fici, 2015). Among schools of thought of social enterprise, some of them, especially those rooted in the cooperative tradition, pay particular attention to democratic ownership structure. The latter is often implemented through a one-member-one-vote rule (rather than one-share-one- vote). In other cases, this constraint implies at least that the voting rights in the governing body with the ultimate decision-making power are not distributed according to capital shares alone (Defourny and Nyssens, 2010, 2017: chapter 6).

Social enterprises, such as community-supported agriculture, energy cooperatives, or circular economy-based businesses, have emerged throughout the world as pioneers in promoting sustainability transitions. They seek to bring about societal change. They do so, however, not through protest or interest-based lobbying, but by organizing processes for learning and experimentation with lifestyle changes and economic production practices. In particular, they aim to produce goods and services that satisfy a broad set of sustainability values, beyond a focus on material and technical progress only, which characterizes many of the individual consumer-oriented market innovations.

International research, especially within the European EMES network, finds that in order to protect the societal mission of these enterprises from the risk of co-optation by market players, specific governance mechanisms should be established. Whereas a main constraint of the conventional capitalistic enterprise is to distribute surplus to the company shareholders, social enterprises have promoted a broad set of alternative governance principles. Prominent features discussed in this section are limits on the distribution of surplus, shareholder structures that give greater weight to long-lasting members (instead of external shareholders), involvement of stakeholders in the decision-making processes, or the mobilization of non-market resources in support of the societal mission. As such, these innovations provide a test-bed for the design of an alternative corporate structure that is not solely driven by market-led material growth.

In contrast to these means for embedding the mission into the governance structure, some capitalistic enterprises that pledge to be mission-driven have neither special profit distribution rules nor democratic decision-making procedures. Rather, they adopt the traditional legal form of a commercial company without any type of constraints, while looking for "triple bottom line" optimization, through balancing social impact, environmental impact, and the remuneration of shareholders. In such cases, there is no guarantee that the social mission will remain at the centre of the decision-making, especially in a highly competitive environment that pushes towards market-oriented profit maximization. Therefore, only those enterprises with capitalistic decision rules that have very clear surplus redistribution rules for the social mission might be considered as truly mission-driven. Table 5.2 (general categories) and Table 5.3 (the general categories with sub-types) provide a schematic representation of these different forms of mission-driven enterprises, based on a meta-analysis that we made of large-scale comparative research on social economy organizations (Defourny and Nyssens, 2017; Lambert et al., 2019).

Embedding the social mission in the organizational rules and mechanisms is of course important, but it is insufficient to successfully upscale social economy organizations. For this, it is the whole environment in which they operate that must change. Scholars of transition theory speak in that regard of experimental niche innovations operating in so-called protected environments, shielding them from an increasingly fierce and globalized market competition (Grin et al., 2010: chapter 5 of part I). Protected niches can provide the necessary space for a path-breaking technology or a radical social innovation to evolve into a more mature form and eventually inspire other transition actors.

Table 5.2 Features of different categories of economic actors (economic features, social dimensions, and governance)

		Public sector	Associations (voluntary sector)	Social enterprises	Capitalistic (for-profit enterprises)
Economic features	Continued production of goods and services	1	1	1	1
	Economic risk taking	0	0	1	1
	Some minimal level of paid employment	1	1/0	1	1
Social dimension	Societal purpose	1	1	1	0
	Civil society anchorage	0	1	1/0	0
	Social use of surplus: limits on distribution to shareholders	1	1	1/0	0
	Mobilization of non-market resources (voluntary labour/subsidies)	1	1	1	0
Governance structure	High degree of autonomy in regards to external investors (self-determination of the governance structure)	0	1	1	0
	Capitalistic decision rules (allocation of votes in accordance with the ownership of shares)	0	0	1/0	1
	Stakeholder/beneficiaries participation in the project	1/0	1	1/0	0
	Residual control rights reside with the members or the founder only	0	1	1	0

Source: Table by the authors. Content based on a meta-analysis of the research results by Defourny and Nyssens (2017: chapter 6).
Legend: 1 = strongly so, 0 = very weakly so, 1/0 = not clear/high degree of diversity on this criterion.
Notes: As regards social enterprises, they have been coded 1/0 with respect to the use of surplus, since although cooperatives are usually categorized as social enterprises on the basis of the democratic decision rules, many do apply limits on the distribution of profits to the shareholders. As regards capitalistic decision rules, the code 1/0 has been applied to social enterprises since capitalistic forms of decision-making can still emphasize the social mission by the imposition of limits on profit distribution (for details, see Table 5.3).

Table 5.3 Various forms of economic entities and associated characteristics

		State-owned enterprises	Associations (voluntary sector)			Social enterprise
		General interest association	Association club	Entrepreneurial association	Public/private social enterprise	Social cooperative (legal status)
Decision rules	Bureaucratic	*				*
	Democratic (one person, one vote)		*	*	*	
	Independent Capitalistic (allocation of votes in accordance with the ownership of shares)					
Surplus distribution	Not authorized	*			*	*
	Limited distribution and asset lock			*		*
	Limited distribution					
	No Limits					
Residual control	State	*				*
	Members non-investors: for society at large		*		*	*
	Members non-investors: for the members			*		
	Investors: founders (non-stocks)					

			Capitalistic (for-profit enterprises)		
Social business-YUNUS	Social business-SME	Social business within corporation	Pocheko model	Capitalistic no stocks	Capitalistic with stocks
*					
		*			
	*	*	*	*	*
	*			*	
*		*	*		
		*	*		
				*	*
*	*	*	*		
*					
				*	*

(*Continued*)

	State-owned enterprises	Associations (voluntary sector)			Social enterprise
	General interest association	Association club	Entrepreneurial association	Public/private social enterprise	Social cooperative (legal status)
Investors: mix founders (non-stocks)- private equity Investors: mixed stocks- founders- private equity Investors: stocks					

Source: Table by the authors, using categories adapted from Defourny and Nyssens (2017: chapter 6) and Lambert et al. (2019).

Legend:
Columns
Column 4: Entrepreneurial association: a non-profit association that relies primarily on market resources (commercial transactions), in contrast to the usual non-profit association that relies on a mix of resources (donations, voluntary labour, and market resources).
Column 5: Public/private social enterprise: social enterprise under public control/public regulation.
Column 7: Social business Yunus type: cost recovery through market resources, all surplus reinvested in supporting the social mission.
Column 10: Social business following the Pocheko model: cost recovery through market resources, all surplus reinvested in the activities of the company implementing a triple bottom line (economic, social and environmental).
Column 9: Social business within the corporation: refers to the new legal forms in the United States (adopted *inter alia* by Patagonia), such as Benefit Corporation, low-profit limited liability corporation, flexible purpose corporation.

Capitalistic (for-profit enterprises)

Social business-YUNUS	Social business-SME	Social business within corporation	Pocheko model	Capitalistic no stocks	Capitalistic with stocks
		*	*		*
			*		*
			*		*

Column 11: Capitalistic no stocks: includes also cooperatives (shares exchanged only amongst the members, they are not freely transferable on the market).

Lines

Asset lock: prevents the distribution of residual rents to members, so that assets of the organizations cannot be used for individual gain and be diverted from the social mission purposes of the organization.

Residual control: this criterion refers to the question of whether it is the stakeholder or the shareholder who allocate the residual income, which is the income that is not assigned by contract to other stakeholders than those who ultimately control the organization (for instance in the case of a bankruptcy or a termination of an organization):

- in a general interest association, the residual income is allocated to general interest purposes (through a donation to another general interest association for instance);
- in an association club, it will be distributed amongst the members;
- in small businesses, it will be allocated to the investors, who can be the founders, private equity, or stockholders.

The relationship of niche experimentation to broader socio-ecological transformation remains ambiguous, however. Some socio-technological transition approaches based on change through small-scale niche innovations seem to pay scant attention to the role of the broader political context, perhaps underestimating the need for the regime to co-evolve with the innovative practices, in order to overcome the various lock-ins that obstruct regime change (Schot and Geels, 2008). This is also what we referred to when discussing the risks entailed with the scenarios of co-optation or of the marginalization of initiatives seeking to promote sociodiversity: we emphasized that the distinction between the different scenarios, in most cases, can be traced back to the receptiveness of the regime to change, and in particular to the adoption by the incumbent actors of a new set of values, and to governance structures that genuinely allow a form of power sharing with the new entrants. Niches can only thrive and develop into alternatives to the mainstream if the political and legal regime opens up opportunities for societal change. Such changes in the political and legal regimes depend in particular on broader socio-cultural changes (Grin et al., 2010: 331).

As we see it, the challenge is twofold. It is first to promote experimental niches that can contribute to the provision of collective goods and services in the context of market activities, without however being fully exposed to market competition. It is, second, to stimulate a broader process of social learning across all spheres of society, and possibly including lifestyle changes. This dual challenge can best be met by embedding social enterprises in social networks that promote a strong social transformation agenda (Dedeurwaerdere et al., 2017). Unlike the narrower category of community enterprises or local economies, these social networks that link social enterprises to one another and to other transition initiatives are not necessarily local, and they are not directed to any specific community. Rather, they combine innovative forms of non-State collective action to deliver collective goods and services, with explicit aspirations for fostering social learning on broader societal transformations (Kunze and Becker, 2015: 435).

Proposal #3: De-financialization of the economy and sustainable finance

Any transition away from the extractive economy requires that investments be channelled towards businesses that adopt sustainable practices: the High-Level Expert Group on Sustainable Finance established by the European Commission describes "short-termism" in its final report as "a clear challenge and potential obstacle for the establishment of a sustainable financial system" (EC, 2018: 47). Yet, although the excesses of financial shareholder capitalism are not only bad for the environment but also for the economy itself – they lead to the emergence of "bubbles" and to the growth of inequalities –, the practices typical of predatory capitalism persist. Such practices include the increase in CEO's compensation resulting in what, quoting from Lazonick (2016), UNCTAD refers to as the emergence of the "value-extracting CEO" (UNCTAD, 2017: 138) or the use of redistribution of the company's surplus to maximize the return for the shareholders. Far from receding, such practices have increased in recent under the pressure of the financial markets.

According to a 2005 survey, "78% of executives feel pressure to sacrifice long-term value to meet earnings targets" (ibid.). In the same vein, a 2013 McKinsey and Canada Pension Plan Investment Board (CPPIB) survey of over 1,000 board members and executives found that that 63% of respondents said the pressure to generate strong short-term results had increased over the previous five years, and 79% felt especially pressured to demonstrate strong financial performance over a period of just two years or less; yet, 86% of the respondents stated that if they had a longer time horizon to make business decisions, "this would positively affect corporate performance in a number of ways, including strengthening financial returns and increasing innovation" (Barton and Wiseman, 2014).

Efforts are underway, in the EU in particular, to define precise criteria for "sustainable finance", in order to encourage socially responsible investment. A major challenge however is that sustainable investment opportunities in the real economy are often insufficient: prominent new sustainable banking initiatives, such as the Dutch bank Triodos, even though they have been able to mobilize substantial capital resources, still find it difficult to invest their available capital resources in existing sustainable businesses which have long-term sustainability at their core.

The move towards a sustainable finance system shall therefore only be possible in combination with a reform of the financial shareholder capitalism model of the firm. As underlined by the High-Level Expert Group,

> more fundamentally, a significant aspect of short-termism in financial markets—and indeed the real economy—has its roots in the frequent separation of the behavior of some financial intermediaries from the preferences of the ultimate beneficiaries. The

best interests of the ultimate beneficiary – savings for pension purposes, for example – may be best served by maximising returns over a lengthy period. But the relevant time horizon for the individual influencing or making the investment decisions can be much more short-term focused. Job tenure and financial rewards for analysts, asset/money managers and traders can be heavily dependent on short-term returns. And some shareholders and managers of companies, especially if they are rewarded by shares/share options, might become influenced by short- term strength in the share price rather than its sustainability over many years.

The financial shareholder model has become dominant globally after having developed in the United States in the 1980s and 1990s. Alternative models of capitalism exist, however. Companies in Germany, Scandinavia, and Japan, for instance, are structured (both in corporate law and in the corporate culture) as institutions accountable to a wide set of stakeholders, including through workers' unions or company bankruptcy laws specifying who gets what in case of bankruptcy (Stiglitz, 2012: 58; cf. illustrations in Table 4). These companies remain capitalist and profit-driven, but the explicit and implicit codes under which they operate are strikingly different. Firms within these countries typically invest more in innovation than their counterparts, which are focused on short-term shareholder value maximization, and the gap between executive pay and the pay of average employees is much more narrow (Jacobs and Mazzucato, 2016: 19). This illustrates the many variations within capitalism: rather than capitalism as a system responding to certain universally applicable laws derived from the profit-seeking motive that animates its agents, what we see in the real world is a broad range of models, depending on legal and policy frameworks, but also on different cultures, relationships to workers' unions, and actors' motivations.

Nevertheless, even in those countries where societal stakeholders have a larger influence on economic decision-making, globalization has led to the relative decline of their influence. Well-documented examples of this trend are the decline in the trade unions' bargaining power through offshoring of certain segments of the production process and the absence of consideration for environmental and social conditions in international trade agreements (De Schutter, 2015a). Globalization, in essence, makes it easier for companies to pollute where environmental regulations are lax or underenforced, to locate the most labour-intensive segments of the production chain where wages are repressed and unions weak, and even to declare profits, if at all, where corporate taxes are low.

The reform of the financial system for ecological and social transition shall operate in sharp contrast to the reductionist approach of financial shareholder capitalism. Its challenge is to adopt a truly interdisciplinary multilevel approach that focuses on a broader set of human well-being outcomes. It is to constitute a bulwark against the pressures towards maximizing short-term profits based on increasing consumption of private goods and the exploitation of natural resources. Both the quality of the environment and the quality of the social and emotional environment have strongly declined over the last three decades in the OECD countries, in spite of overall sustained economic growth, expressed in GDP per capita (Bartolini and Sarracino, 2014). Various forms of capital – natural, human and social – have been eroded, and neither the growth of physical capital (infrastructures) nor the increase of financial capital (captured by a narrow elite at the top) can be seen to compensate for that loss.

Investment in these non-material dimensions of well-being (in natural, human and social capital) can be done both in corporations and social enterprises for instance through investing in civic education and participation, contributing to the preservation and access to natural environments, and in workers' overall well-being. While these investments may seem costly in the short term, they are an essential ingredient of long-term prosperity. Increased subjective well-being makes people more productive at work (Flint-Taylor and Cooper, 2014). It also decreases the costs of welfare policies (Eriksson and Lindström, 2014). Further, various studies show that higher degrees of workers' participation in the enterprise – what is often referred to as economic democracy – improves both the firms' economic performance (Breza et al., 2018) and levels of civic engagement and democratic decision making in society as a whole (Ferreras, 2017). For instance, scholars of the German corporate governance system (the well-known *Mittbestimmung* model) have shown that judicious use of labour representation on the company's supervisory board allows to better take into account the workers' well-being concerns, while also bringing valuable operational knowledge to the boards' decision making (Fauver and Fuerst, 2006): the Hans Böckler Foundation published various studies showing that companies operating according to co-determination perform better economically, provide better long-term training to the employees, ensure better job security, include a larger proportion of women on surveillance boards, and are better at integrating long-term considerations related to sustainability in their strategic decisions.

While these investments in natural, human and social capital contribute only indirectly to productivity growth, they make a direct contribution to socially just and environmentally sustainable well-being. Companies prioritizing investments in these well-being dimensions typically do not generate the double-digit return on investment that financial markets tend to see as the holy grail. But they may be a real contribution to improved human well-being.

Social movements, citizens, and forward-looking policy makers now understand the importance of reorienting capital flows in the direction of organizations and companies that contribute such investments for the benefit of society as a whole. A new generation of financial institutions such as social and environmental banking systems or social investment cooperatives is now emerging, responding to these societal expectations. Triodos Bank was established in the Netherlands in 1980. Along with its European branches, it has initiated an approach to banking with two features that break with the dominant rules of the financial system. First, the bank only lends money that the bank effectively received from savings or investors (in contrast to the dominant practices of banks who artificially create money by lending a five to ten times multiple of what they receive). Second, the bank only supports projects with clear cultural, social, or environmental benefits. Even though the returns are not as high as regular commercial banking, the bank generated in 2016 over 200 million euros of surplus, which shows the financial sustainability of the business model they pioneered.

Another example is the French cooperative investment fund based in Paris, SPEAR. This innovative fund has developed financial tools to combine a direct monitoring of the social return on investment, in addition to the financial return. SPEAR screens a set of projects that are potentially relevant in the neighbourhood of its members that potentially provide a high social, cultural or environmental return on the community. It then publicizes these projects through an online portal for the members. Individuals and organizations that wish to invest acquire a share in this cooperative investment fund and indicate the project which they would like their investment to support. In return, SPEAR negotiates with their partners in the banking sector a credit to these projects and a fair financial return to the investors.

In both of these examples, corporate structures have been set up with a view to embedding the societal mission to a maximum extent into the long-term functioning of the organization, and creating various forms of "integrity shields" to avoid institutional drift. In the case of SPEAR, the initiators have established a cooperative structure, so that the control remains in the hands of the members of the cooperative through democratic decision rules. In the case of Triodos, external investors are hosted in a separate organizational entity (the "Foundation for the Administration of Triodos Bank Shares" (SAAT)), so that external financial investors cannot directly influence the decision making of the Triodos bank itself, where the decision making remains in the hands of the founders who protect the societal mission of the company. Thus, the institutional environment matters. The responsibility of the enabling State is to establish such institutional frameworks supporting more sustainable ways of doing business and to guide investors towards such actors.

Proposal #4: Changing public action: from the Captive State to the Enabling State

Because it requires a change in lifestyles – in our ways of producing and consuming, in our mobility and housing routines –, transition in a post-growth society requires the creation of spaces in which the re-creation of norms by the individual should again become a real possibility. The classic forms of representative democracy and of responsible consumption shall not suffice. In our complex societies, characterized both by multilevel governance and by the lengthening of production chains – the result of a deepening of the division of labour –, individuals can only bring about limited changes through the ballot and the wallet – as voters and as consumers, taking part in elections and acting as responsible purchasers of goods and services. Instead, escaping the current post-war growth model means for each individual the ability to challenge the social norms in the web of which he or she is caught: individual autonomy is only plausible if combined with collective autonomy, that is, with a questioning of the inherited norms and the conceptions of "success" or "happiness" that such norms embody.

If this diagnosis is correct, important consequences follow for the shape of public action. First, the self-organization of civil society initiatives should be supported. In order to foster the transition, based on grassroots social innovation, public action needs to focus on the creativity of social actors and their desire to invest in the construction of collective action. Such a form of intervention stands on a delicate ridge. It must support without imposing. It must abandon the idea of "commanding" the transition or of setting the pace, but it must create the conditions for the emergence of initiatives led by an individual or several individuals acting together. Such public action must promote local diversity and experimentation, but at the same time ensure that initiatives are networked so that good practices can spread more rapidly, that there is some mutualization between them, and that these practices contribute to an overall territorial evolution.

Second, local decision-making should be encouraged, favouring experimentation. The revitalization of local democracy stimulates the search for new solutions: veto points are fewer at that level, and the possibilities of synergies between different policy areas are greater (McKibben, 2007). Local democracy thus could favour overcoming the division between the "decision-makers" and the "decision-receivers", bringing the policy choices closer to the preoccupations of those in the name of whom they are adopted. Similarly, the strengthening of "civil society" (i.e., of the full range of associations in which individuals seek, on a voluntary basis, to contribute to civic life) allows each individual to build social links based on shared convictions and of a common will for change, and thus to take part in collective actions.

The emphasis on rebuilding of social capital at the local level is not of course to favour a return to the communitarianism of the past, one in which individual choices are determined by the birth circumstances of each individual. In traditional societies, these circumstances typically define the individual's role in the division of social labour as well as the solidarity mechanisms he or she could rely on through the "proximate protection" – from family members, from the community of neighbours, or from the profession he or she belongs to. Nothing could be further from what we have in min. Our hope is, rather, that each member of the society shall have an opportunity to co-construct with others certain alternatives, and thereby to invent new ways of life – new ways of moving, of eating, or of working –, escaping from the standardization of modern society.

This utopia is already part of our daily experience. At the scale of the neighbourhood, of the school, or of the town, ordinary citizens permanently innovate. They invent new ways of sharing, rescuing a certain idea of the "commons" that was once thought to be definitely relegated to the past, after the loss of traditional forms of solidarity and the growth of a hyper-individualistic society in which the position of each individual seems to be defined by his or her consumption. They put in place tools that allow relocalization of economic relationships, breathing new life in local exchange systems, and encouraging a reliance on local currencies to maximize the impacts on the local economy of market exchanges. In the areas of energy, transport, or food, they encourage new ways of producing and consuming. They score twice: they try to reduce their ecological footprint – often succeeding in doing so – at the same time that they seek to strengthen the links between individuals, thus combating social exclusion (AEIDL, 2013; Dervojeda et al., 2013).

In the setting up of these so-called "citizens' initiatives", the process matters as much as the end result. These initiatives aim, of course, at the "energy descent" (a concept initially coined by economists Odum and Odum (Odum and Odum, 2001: 4)), and at building more resilient local communities, better equipped to resist to shocks, whether economic or natural, by nurturing a diversity of local resources. But they also seek to affirm, at the micro-political level of cultural practices and of social relationships, requirements of democracy and participation that elevate each individual, really, as the co-author of his or her environment. Autonomy should mean not only the capacity to shape alternatives, but also the ability to question the dominant representation of the motivations of actors.

The revitalization of local democracy and the strengthening of civil society go hand in hand to strengthen the potential for citizens-led initiatives: such initiatives shall only be able to emerge, and be sustained, if they can be supported by hybrid governance mechanisms involving ordinary citizens, private economic actors, and public authorities, in the design and the implementation of alternatives. However, just like we should avoid falling into the trap of thinking that society is made of a single cloth so that change could only be conceived of as radical and as bringing about a complete replacement of one system by another, we should guard ourselves against the exact opposite illusion. Local alternatives shall only have lasting impacts and gradually spread across society, if they are supported (and their dissemination encouraged) by levels of governance that are not solely local.

A third condition for social innovation to be able to flourish is therefore that we move beyond the local. At the higher levels of governance, what is needed is a change in the dominant culture of governance. Since Plato's *Republic*, which placed its fate in the hands of the Philosopher-Kings and their expert wisdom, the task of politics has traditionally been thought of as having to think for society, and to impose on society certain solutions, as it were, "from above". In such a scheme, it is almost inevitable that local diversity and the specificity of the contexts in which regulatory and policy frameworks are implemented shall be negated – eradicated if possible, or at least perceived as a problem to be overcome. After all, if a solution is deemed desirable because it is the most rational, or seen as the one that best serves the general interest, why should it not be generalized across society?

It is this very scheme that we must now put into question, and it is this task of politics that should now give way to another. For politics should not be homogenizing per necessity. Instead, it could recast itself as serving local initiatives, thus allowing them to flourish by removing the constraints that are obstacles to their growth and dissemination. The role of higher levels of governance, in this view, should not only be to manage the externalities. It should also be to design the framework within which the local initiatives develop so as to allow these initiatives to grow, by setting up enabling mechanisms – mechanisms which allow supporting the diversity of social innovations by adapting the legal and economic institutions which facilitate their establishment and their further development. Finally, higher levels of governance should accelerate collective learning, encouraging each local entity to gain from the experiments led by other local entities, both as a source of inspiration and as a means to enhance accountability.

Proposal #5: Changing behavioural motivations: from mandates to experiments

The transition to a society that ranks other objectives (such as well-being, or real freedom understood as the expansion of its members' capabilities) above economic growth, shall not be effected all at once; nor shall it be achieved by relying only on the limited range of instruments – regulatory reforms or economic incentives – that the State may use. Social psychology has highlighted the limited impact of such instruments, which impose on individuals injunctions that rely on "extrinsic" motivations (Ryan and Deci, 2000a, 2000b; Moller et al., 2006), and thus treat individuals like objects rather than as subjects of their own history (Arendt, 1958). Individuals on whom rules are imposed, to whom subsidies are promised, or who are threatened with having to pay taxes, will act in order to comply with the rule, to capture the subsidy, or to avoid paying the tax – but they will otherwise pursue their own life objectives, deviating as little as possible from such objectives that they have set for themselves. Nor is a single focus on knowledge sharing and creating awareness sufficient to stimulate action. We argue here that in order to stimulate responsible behaviour, mechanisms should be established to ensure reflexivity, sociability, and agency.

We start by noting that, in contrast with the imposition of mandates or economic incentives, behavioural changes that rely on the intrinsic motivations of the individual shall be resilient: because these changes are based on the individual's identity or self-image or on the values that the individual treats as his/her own, such changes will persist in time, even though the context (and the external incentives it provides) may have evolved. This is true, in particular, as regards pro-environmental behaviour (Lavergne et al., 2010). Moreover, as individuals seek to design solutions in the immediate environment in which they operate, responding to the ecological crisis by inventing new ways of producing and of consuming, new lifestyles, new economic models, a collective search commences. Solutions are tested, and they can gradually grow into new social norms solidifying, which can be diffused from individual to individual before being generalized across society and replace existing routines.

This is democratic experimentalism. Social innovations that have been successfully experimented with in some settings have an empowering effect throughout society. By referring to successful experiments, others, operating in other fora or in other jurisdictions, can more easily demand from decision-makers that they consider such experiments and that they create the legal and economic institutions that may favour their emergence. Of course, proposing to create "spontaneous", "citizens-led" social innovations by operating from above, is about as contradictory as proposing to fasten the growth of a tree by pulling on its branches: ultimately, if there is no appetite for the social innovation in question, encouraging its diffusion shall lead, at best, to changes on a limited scale and that may be short-lived.

Therefore, the establishment of enabling mechanisms for such innovations, together with a deliberate attempt to learn from what has worked elsewhere, will depend on the appetite for reflexive learning on transitions' objectives, and for taking part in existing social action within given groups and communities (so-called sociability) and the development of individual democratic agency at various levels.

First, in order to move towards a society that escapes the trap of growth, a learning process is required that challenges the overall normative orientation of the societal transformation processes. Such reflexive social learning challenges our deeper beliefs about what is desirable, our representation of ourselves (Swieringa and Wierdsma, 1992; Peschl, 2008). Indeed, transition calls for a reflexive process of social learning: we need to revisit the fundamental question of how each individual defines his or her understanding of the "good life", and at the societal level, the question of the trajectory that we wish to pursue collectively.

Second, social innovation thrives upon sociability and agency, i.e. the active involvement of citizens at all levels of society (within associations, the works sphere, local politics, etc.). Uitto's research (2015) points out that participatory activities significantly influence the involvement of actors in societal transformation. At a first level, Uitto documented the importance of sociability, which are participatory activities leading the individual to take part in existing social action. This first level is easily accessible to all and might stimulate the involvement of new actors in change processes. At a second level, building upon the involvement in these general pro-social activities, actors can be invited to become more active agents by taking responsibility or leadership roles at various levels of social organization. For instance, recent research on primary school education shows that, to be effective, education on sustainable development should not only provide exposure to ecological experiences but should also, even more importantly, connect pupils to pro-social and agency activities through an approach that emphasizes pro-environmental values and self-efficacy in taking part in ecological behaviour (Uitto et al., 2015).

The promotion of sociability and agency within organizations and communities will require investing in a broad set of enabling governance mechanisms (which might or might not depend on State support). As can be seen from the discussion above, the agency doesn't stand separately from sociability: instead, it overlaps with sociability, which it develops into a higher, more intense form. Therefore, one can consider three different levels, from weak sociability (level 1) to strong sociability (level 2) to agency (level 3; Figure 5.2).

Figure 5.3 illustrates some of these mechanisms in the case of mission-driven organizations of the sharing economy in Brussels, showing the progression from weak sociability to the agency in six organizations. These organizations come from the sector of car sharing (Tappaz and Cozycar); sharing of electric scooters (Scooty), sharing of garage space for selling locally produced food baskets (Gasap), garden sharing (Samentuinen), room sharing (Couchsurfing), and co-housing (Communa). Examples promoting weak sociability are the setting up of local sustainability initiatives or face to face encounters between users and producers; strong sociability can

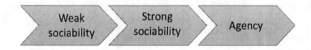

Figure 5.2 Weak sociability limits itself to actions where social connections are made in order to discuss or raise awareness on societal issues. The level of strong sociability is reached when these actions lead to a cooperative activity or mutual involvement. At the agency level finally, citizens take up an active role, set their own goals, and act upon them (Benkler, 2006).

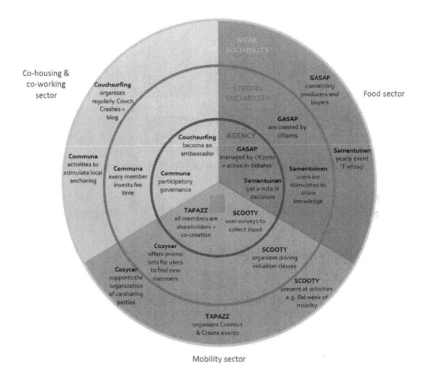

Figure 5.3 Listing of governance mechanisms to foster sociability and agency in social mission-driven organizations of the sharing economy in Brussels.

Source: Brabant and Dedeurwaerdere (2017).

be promoted by actively sharing knowledge or involving users to find new members amongst others; agency finally can be promoted by opportunities for participation in debates or in decision making; and involvement in the management or becoming an active ambassador of an organization.

References

AEIDL (European Association of local development initiatives - Association européenne des initiatives de développement local). (2013). *Europe in Transition: Local Communities Leading the Way to a Low-Carbon Society.* Retreived online: http://www.socioeco.org/bdf_fiche-document-2014_en.html
Arendt, H. (1958). *The Human Condition.* Chicago: University of Chicago Press.

Bartolini, S. and Sarracino, F. (2014). *The Dark Side of Chinese Growth: Explaining Decreasing Well-being in Times of Economic Boom*. World Congress of Sociology Facing an Unequal World.

Barton, D. and Wiseman, M. (2014). Focusing Capital on the Long Term. *Harvard Business Review*, *92*(1/2): 44–51.

Benkler, Y. and Nissenbaum, H. (2006). Commons-based peer production and virtue. *Journal of Political Philosophy*, *14*(4): 394–419.

Brabant, K. and Dedeurwaerdere, T. (2017). Can the sharing economy realize responsible citizenship behavior? LPTransition Transdisciplinary research briefs on the sharing economy series #1. Retrieved online: https://lptransition.uclouvain.be/downloads/publications/Policy%20brief-nr1.pdf

Breza, E., Kaur, S. and Shamdasani, Y. (2018). The morale effects of pay inequality. *The Quarterly Journal of Economics*, *133*(2): 611–663.

Chell, E. (2007). Social enterprise and entrepreneurship: Towards a convergent theory of the entrepreneurial process. *International Small Business Journal*, *25*: 5–26.

Dedeurwaerdere, T., De Schutter, O., Hudon, M., Mathijs, E., Annaert, B., Avermaete, T., Bleeckx, Th., de Callataÿ, C., De Snijder, P., Fernández-Wulff, P., Joachain, H., and Vivero, J. L. (2017). The governance features of social enterprise and social network activities of collective food buying groups. *Ecological Economics*, *140*: 123–135.

Defourny, J. and Nyssens, M. (2010). Conceptions of social enterprise and social entrepreneurship in Europe and the United States: Convergences and divergences. *Journal of Social Entrepreneurship*, *1*: 32–53.

Defourny, J. and Nyssens, M. (2017). *Economie sociale et solidaire*. Louvain-la-Neuve: De Boeck.

Dervojeda, K., Verzijl, D., Nagtegaal, F., Lengton, M., Rouwmaat, E., Monfardini, E. and Frideres, L. (2013). The sharing economy. *Accessibility Based Business Models for Peer-to-Peer Markets*. Business Innovation Observatory. Case Study 12. European Commission, DG Enterprise and Industry.

De Schutter, O. (2015a). *Trade in the Service of Sustainable Development. Linking Trade to Labour Rights and Environmental Standards*. Oxford and New York: Bloomsbury/Hart.

EC (2018). *Financing a Sustainable European Economy. Final Report*, 47. European Commission: EU High-Level Group on Sustainable Finance.

Eriksson, M. and Lindström, B. (2014). The salutogenic framework for well-being: Implications for public policy. In Timo, J. H. and Michaelson, J. (eds.). *Well-Being and Beyond*: 68–97. Cheltenham: Edward Elgar Publishing.

Fauver, L. and Fuerst, M.E. (2006). Does good corporate governance include employee representation? Evidence from German corporate boards. *Journal of Financial Economics*, *82*(3): 673–710.

Ferreras, I. (2017). *Firms as Political Entities: Saving Democracy through Economic Bicameralism*. Cambridge, MA: Cambridge University Press.

Fici, A. (2015). Recognition and legal forms of social enterprise in Europe: A critical analysis from a comparative law perspective. *European Business Law Review*, 27(5): 639–667.

Flint-Taylor, J. and Cooper, C.L. (2014). Well-being in organizations. In Timo, J. H. and Michaelson, J. (eds.). *Well-Being and Beyond*: 244–270. Cheltenham: Edward Elgar Publishing.

Grin, J., Rotmans, J. and Schot, J. (2010). *Transitions to Sustainable Development.* Abingond-on-Thames: Routledge.

Herrero, P., Dedeurwaerdere, T. and Osinski, A. (2018). Design features of social learning in transformative transdisciplinary research. *Sustainability Science, 15*(2): 1–19.

Hirsch Hadorn, G., Hoffmann-Riem, H., Biber-Klemm, S., Grossenbacher-Mansuy, W., Joye, D., Pohl, C., Wiesmann, U. and Zemp, E. (eds.) (2008). *Handbook of Transdisciplinary Research*. Berlin and Heidelberg: Springer.

Jacobs, M. and Mazzucato, M. (eds.). (2016). *Rethinking Capitalism: Economics and Policy for Sustainable and Inclusive Growth*. Hoboken: John Wiley & Sons.

Jahn, T., Bergmann, M. and Keil, F. (2012). Transdisciplinarity: Between mainstreaming and marginalization. *Ecological Economics, 79*: 1–10.

Johanisova, N., Crabtree, T. and Frankova, E. (2013). Social enterprises and non-market capitals: A path to degrowth? *Journal of Cleaner Production, 38*: 7–16.

Kuhlmann, S. and Rip, A. (2014). *The Challenge of Addressing Grand Challenges*. European Research and Innovation Board. Retrieved online: https://research.utwente.nl/files/5140568/The_challenge_of_addressing_Grand_Challenges.pdf

Kunze, C. and Becker, S. (2015). Collective ownership in renewable energy and opportunities for sustainable degrowth. *Sustainability Science, 10*(3): 425–437.

Lambert, L., Dedeurwaerdere, T., Nyssens, M., Severi, E. and Brolis, O. (2019). Unpacking the organisational diversity within the collaborative economy: The contribution of an analytical framework from social enterprise theory. *Ecological Economics, 164*: 1–9.

Lang, D.J., Wiek, A., Bergmann, M., Stauffacher, M., Martens, P., Moll, P., Swilling, M. and Thomas, C. (2012). Transdisciplinary research in sustainability science: Practice, principles, and challenges. *Sustainability Science, 7*(1): 25–43.

Larsson, J. and Bolin, L. (2014). *Low-Carbon Gothenburg 2.0: Technological Potentials and Lifestyle Changes*. Mistra Urban Futures. Retrieved online: https://www.mistraurbanfutures.org/en/publication/low-carbon-gothenburg-20-technological-potentials-and-lifestyle-changes

Lavergne, K.J., Sharp, E., Pelletier, L.G. and Holtby, A. (2010). The role of perceived government style in the facilitation of self-determined and non self-determined motivation for pro-environmental behavior. *Journal of Environmental Psychology, 30*(2): 169–177.

Lazonick, W. (2016). The value-extracting CEO: How executive stock-based pay undermines investment in productive capabilities. Working Paper No. 54, Institute for New Economic Thinking (INET), Oxford.

McKibben, B. (2007), *Deep Economy: The Wealth of Communities and the Durable Future*. New York: Henry Holt & Co.

Moller, A.C., Ryan, R.M. and Deci, E. (2006). Self-determination theory and public policy: Improving the quality of consumer decisions without using coercion. *Journal of Public Policy and Marketing*, 25(1): 104–116.

Odum, H.T. and Odum, E.C. (2001). *A Prosperous Way Down*. Boulder: University Press of Colorado.

OECD (2020). Addressing societal challenges using transdisciplinary research. *OECD Science, Technology and Industry Policy Papers*, 88, OECD Publishing.

Peschl, M.F. (2008). Triple-loop learning as foundation for profound change, individual cultivation, and radical innovation: Construction processes beyond scientific and rational knowledge. Munich Personal RePEc Archive, No. 9940.

Ryan, R.M. and Deci, E.L. (2000a). Intrinsic and extrinsic motivations: Classic definitions and new directions. *Contemporary Educational Psychology*, 25: 54–67.

Ryan, R.M. and Deci, E.L. (2000b). Self-determination theory and the facilitation of intrinsic motivation, social development, and well-being. *American Psychologist*, 55(1): 68–78.

Schot, J. and Geels, F.W. (2008). Strategic niche management and sustainable innovation journeys: Theory, findings, research agenda, and policy. *Technology Analysis & Strategic Management*, 20(5): 537–554.

Seyfang, G. and Smith, A. (2007). Grassroots innovations for sustainable development: Towards a new research and policy agenda. *Environmental Politics*, 16(4): 584–603.

Stamm, A., Dantas, E., Fischer, D., Ganguly, S. and Rennkamp, B. (2009). Sustainability-oriented innovation systems: Towards decoupling economic growth from environmental pressures? Discussion Paper of the German Development Institute, No. 20.

Stiglitz, J.E. (2012). *The Price of Inequality: How Today's Divided Society Endangers Our Future*. New York: WW Norton & Company.

Swieringa, J. and Wierdsma, A. (1992). *Becoming a Learning Organization*. Reading, MA: Addison-Wesley.

Uitto, A., Boeve-de Pauw, J. and Saloranta, S. (2015). Participatory school experiences as facilitators for adolescents' ecological behavior. *Journal of Environmental Psychology*, 43: 55–65.

UNCTAD (United Nations Conference on Trade and Development). (2017). *Beyond Austerity: Towards a Global New Deal: Trade and Development Report 2017*. Geneva.

Weber, K.M. and Rohracher, H. (2012). Legitimizing research, technology and innovation policies for transformative change: Combining insights from innovation systems and multi-level perspective in a comprehensive 'failures' framework. *Research Policy*, 41(6): 1037–1047.

6 The missing Sustainable Development Goal

Enabling social innovations

On 25 September 2015, the Heads of State and governments present at the UN General Assembly adopted the 2030 Development Agenda, pledging to ensure that "no one will be left behind". "We resolve", they stated, by 2030,

> to end poverty and hunger everywhere; to combat inequalities within and among countries; to build peaceful, just and inclusive societies; to protect human rights and promote gender equality and the empowerment of women and girls; and to ensure the lasting protection of the planet and its natural resources. We resolve also to create conditions for sustainable, inclusive and sustained economic growth, shared prosperity and decent work for all, taking into account different levels of national development and capacities.

The 2030 Development Agenda was prepared on the basis of a widely participatory process, in which civil society groups across the world were actively involved. The Sustainable Development Goals are therefore the result of a compromise between the views of governments, and the views expressed by local communities. They include an explicit Target, under SDG 17, related to the building of partnerships with civil society.

Yet, the SDGs remain incomplete. Despite the reference to partnerships with civil society, they are otherwise entirely silent about the potential of citizens-led social innovations to help in achieving the other goals. Moreover, while they include (as part of SDG 17, on revitalizing the global partnership for development) a commitment to "build on existing initiatives to develop measurements of progress on sustainable development that complement gross domestic product", the associated indicators are silent about this objective: these indicators focus

DOI: 10.4324/9781003223542-6

instead on the other part of the Target, which is to "support statistical capacity-building in developing countries". Perhaps even more significant, under SDG 8, which relates to decent work and economic growth, Target 8.1. is to "sustain per capita economic growth in accordance with national circumstances and, in particular, at least 7 per cent gross domestic product growth per annum in the least developed countries"; the associated indicator (8.1.1.), is the annual growth rate of real GDP per capita.

We seem unable to picture a development pathway without growth. This is in part for reasons of political expediency: because post-growth models of development are politically unpopular, they have not been part of the mainstream discussion on the future of societies, despite the robust empirical evidence showing that it is not realistic to pursue growth without increasing both the use of resources and the emissions of greenhouse gases responsible for the heating of the planet (Hickel and Kallis, 2019). But the lack of post-growth models is also a failure of our imagination. We remain prisoners of the "Ecological Modernization Theory", according to which growth is a pre-condition of the adoption of policies that ensure environmental sustainability (see Bergius and Buseth, 2019). Alternatives to this dominant model have been systematically sidelined: in particular, "zero-growth" approaches to environmental sustainability (as illustrated by Daly, 1977 or Offe, 1987) have been marginalized or entirely ignored (Weber and Weber, 2020).

There is a connection between these two deficiencies. It is only by building on social innovations that we can identify means through which the ecological and social transition can be achieved without growth, at least in the rich countries. Indeed, there is a link between the definition of alternative measures of human prosperity and the democratizing and empowering that could result from the promotion of citizens-led social innovations. Happiness of the individual through consumption, and progress of society by the continued improvement of standards of living: it is these representations, or these myths, that are the main obstacles to the active involvement of citizens and social actors in the imagination of alternatives. The *autonomy* of citizen action therefore emerges as a condition for alternatives to emerge, and it is because social innovations may favour such autonomy that the establishment of new modes of governance fostering individual agency is key. Autonomy, indeed, is the ability for the individual as well as for the community to choose the norms by which they shall be guided (Castoriadis, 1975). Its exercise requires that we create the conditions for sufficient reflexivity, allowing both the individual and society to define their long-term goals, and to make choices that shall allow them to make progress towards realizing those objectives.

Assessing progress: from the growth of GDP per capita to "true wealth"

Earlier in this essay, we noted that the persistent insistence on growth, however "greened", is a major obstacle to our ability to drive societies towards a sustainable future (Hickel and Kallis, 2019). But this almost religious devotion to growth (Méda, 2013) as a basis of social progress has deeply rooted explanations. It is premised on the idea that the flourishing of each member of society depends on the constant expansion of the possibilities of material consumption (Scitovsky, 1976; Layard, 2005; Dolan et al., 2008). It is this belief that makes it appear so imperative to strive for an increase in income combined with a reduction of the real price of consumer items, the latter being achieved thanks to the standardization of production, the competition between producers, and market-led technological innovations. This belief may be naïve, however. As Richard Easterlin has noted, increases in GDP has been disconnected from improvements in subjective well-being since the early 1970s: beyond a certain point of material opulence and comfort, he noted, additional improvements do not contribute to the betterment of subjective perceptions of well-being, or what most people call happiness (Easterlin, 1972, 1995; Layard, 2005).

There are a number of reasons for this disconnect (Senik, 2014). First, there is the phenomenon of adaptation. People get used to what they have, and therefore need more than just minor improvements in their comfort levels to be "happy": they need excitement, novelty, or what Tibor Scitovsky called "pleasure" (which he opposed to mere "comfort", an undisturbed state of affairs which very soon turns out to be boring – Scitovsky, 1976). Indeed, this was how Albert Hirschman explained our tolerance for planned obsolescence: might it not have something to do with the fact that durable consumer goods with the longest life shall provide a certain level of "comfort", but only one single shot of "pleasure" (Hirschman, 1982: 32–38)?

Second, many consumer goods in our advanced societies are essentially "positional" in nature: rather than satisfying real needs, they chiefly serve to rank oneself within society, or to achieve social status. As Fred Hirsch remarked in his classic critique of dominant understandings of growth (Hirsch, 1976: 175 and 245–250), this leads to a situation in which the benefits expected from the progress of material wealth, and from its extension to all groups of society thanks to mass production, end up cancelling themselves out. Indeed, positional goods are specific precisely insofar as the value of the good to the individual depends on others not having significantly more of the good: my impressive-looking car is of much lesser value to me if I am in a society in which the vast majority have equally impressive cars, and not just a well-functioning bicycle and a free pass allowing me to take trains (Brighouse and Swift, 2006).

Finally, GDP growth only provides an indication about the wealth created in the economy as a whole, but it is silent about how such wealth is distributed. Yet, the impressive rise of inequalities in all societies since the mid-1980s results in a situation in which, for most people, the proud announcement by political leaders that GDP has increased under their watch (and, of course, thanks to the policies they have put in place), is entirely unrelated to their everyday subjective experience. In other terms, not only is GDP unrelated to well-being or life satisfaction, as experienced by most people: for the vast majority of households in most societies in the world, it also bears little or no relationship to the increase of their own purchasing power, and thus to the improvement even of their material living conditions (Laurent and Le Cacheux, 2015: 23–25).

But there is another side to this discussion on how the growth of GDP per capita relates to subjective well-being or "happiness". Indeed, alternatively, the pursuit of growth may be based on the finding that in a society which is making "progress", one's subjective well-being gains from knowing that, however adverse present life circumstances may be, there is a real hope that the future might bring about improvements. This idea was initially presented by Albert Hirschman and Michael Rothschild in a paper in which they highlighted the "tunnel effect", by reference to the sense of relief a car driver may feel, even when stuck in the traffic, from finding that the lane next to his own is moving forward: to this driver, the fact that others are moving is perceived as an indication that she too, in time, shall benefit from the general progress (Hirschman and Rothschild, 1973). Hirschman and Rothschild explained by this phenomenon the acceptance of high levels of inequality in fast-growing developing economies. Since then, their intuition has been confirmed by empirical studies highlighting the psychological comfort one obtains from projected gains: contrary to what standard economic analysis might have anticipated (in which future gains are more or less heavily discounted), most subjects appear to prefer to move from the least pleasurable to the most pleasurable experiences, because the very anticipation of future improvement is highly valued as a source of subjective well-being (Loewenstein, 1987; see also Senik, 2008).

The debate concerning the relationship of GDP growth to subjective well-being that was provoked by the "Easterlin paradox", therefore, can largely be redescribed as a debate between the respective importance of the various mechanisms at work: while adaptation and social comparisons explain the disconnect between GDP growth and happiness identified in certain studies, even where people do capture some of the benefits from economic progress (that is, where the increase of inequality does not erase its impacts), the "tunnel effect" (the anticipation of future improvements in a society that is in general making progress) may nevertheless partly compensate for this, and people may be "happier" if they believe that their situation shall improve (Senik, 2014).

It is high time that we launch a debate on these issues, and that we identify sources of subjective well-being that do not require the further pursuit of growth in our advanced societies (or that do not require, at least, a form of growth that is not decoupled from resource consumption and pollution). Indeed, our drive for growth has been eroding the natural capital on which all human activity ultimately depends, both as a provider of resources and as a sink to absorb our waste (Daly, 1976). A number of planetary boundaries have already been crossed, and we are already facing an unprecedented ecological crisis resulting from this pursuit.

The societal transformation required to move away from our unsustainable growth model should encourage us to rethink economic prosperity, understood as the extension of the possibilities of material consumption, and to question its rank in our order of priorities: instead of being an end in itself, economic prosperity should become a means in the service of ends that we should choose freely (Cassiers et al., 2011; Thiry, 2017). The burgeoning work by leading scholars and social actors over the last decade on alternative progress indicators and frameworks for safe and just transition can provide an appropriate starting point to guide this collective reflection on redefining prosperity (Jackson, 2009). We cannot change course without first defining an alternative pathway: a vision to follow. Researchers, social movements, and policy makers have already developed a wide array of new approaches to human progress and well-being. These approaches aim to define and assess minimum social and environmental threshold conditions for sustainable progress, and to integrate both material and non-material aspects of human well-being into the definitions of human progress. Important elements of non-material well-being that are considered are access to education and life-long learning for all, social belonging, and mental health, among others.

In spite of major global reports by scholars and international institutions that document the multiple human, natural and social dimensions of the rampant sustainability crisis, this wealth of knowledge is not readily useable to guide sustainability transformations. Indeed, many of these dimensions are not directly measurable and their definition requires a social deliberation over the most relevant criteria to assess improvements in sustainability outcomes (Pelenc and Ballet, 2015). In the absence of such a joint deliberation, "ivory tower" researchers often opt for using more simple measurable features in their models of transition. Classical examples are measurements of the increase in material well-being within the constraints of the planets' resources, or measurements of the increase in the rate of technological innovation that contributes to "cleaner" (more resource-efficient, less polluting) production systems. In order to address the challenges of the transition towards socially just and environmentally sustainable well-being, however, we need a broader set of criteria.

Classic approaches to "sustainable development" see it as a balance to be struck between the social, environmental, and economic dimensions of human development. Such approaches however fail to integrate many of the non-material aspects of human well-being as essential components of sustainability transitions. They also lack a clear concept of critical thresholds of social and environmental unsustainability as a minimum baseline that has to be satisfied before searching for a balance between the other aspects of the social, economic, and environmental dimensions. Indeed, for a number of environmental or social indicators, "tipping points" can be identified, which cannot be crossed without unleashing vicious feedback loops that shall lead to potentially irreversible, and largely unpredictable, consequences (United Nations, 2019: 13). Examples of such tipping points in the environmental area are the melting of the Arctic sea ice (which increases absorption of sunlight by the oceans and thus further accelerates global heating), or the transformation of the Amazonian forest into a savannah (that disturbs rain cycles in the whole region and may lead to further desertification); in the social area, extreme inequality may result in such a "tipping point", as it may result in halting social mobility, so that poverty is transmitted from one generation to the next: inequalities at this point become "self-perpetuating", "for instance through inherited wealth or exclusive access to high-quality education and skills" (United Nations, 2019: 17, citing Corak, 2013 and Chetty et al., 2016).

The "Commission on the Measurement of Economic Performance and Social Progress" established by French President Nicolas Sarkozy in 2009, better known as the Stiglitz-Sen-Fitoussi Commission (Stiglitz et al., 2009), put the issue of a broader approach towards human well-being high on the political agenda. They identified eight basic functionings that allow individuals to live the life that they value. At least in principle, these dimensions should be considered simultaneously in what we may call the multi-dimensional dashboard the report proposes to rely on:

1 Material living standards (income, consumption, and wealth)
2 Health
3 Education
4 Personal activities including work (including the right to a decent job and housing)
5 Political voice (participation in the political process) and governance (constitutional rights, etc.)
6 Social connections and relationships
7 Environment (impact of noise, presence of nature, pollution, etc. on well-being)
8 Insecurity, of an economic as well as a physical nature

By going beyond the traditional focus on the material aspects of human needs (a bias still present in the conventional tri-dimensional sustainability approaches), this multi-dimensional dashboard approach represents a major improvement. It is a useful tool to stimulate societies to consider the full scope of human well-being dimensions, even though the meanings attached to each of these will vary according to the context and culture. However, the dashboard still fails to address the second shortcoming of the conventional sustainability analysis in terms of a balance between a set of criteria. Indeed, before any balancing exercise between various dimensions, there are some minimal baseline criteria to satisfy. The first is fair and equitable access to the decision-making processes that lead to social choices and trade-offs amongst the dimensions. The second is a set of minimum thresholds for the functioning of the Earth's main biophysical regulatory systems in which human beings can flourish. The third is the minimum conditions for enabling the basic functionings that allow individuals to live the life that they value, as for instance analysed in the Stiglitz-Sen-Fitoussi report. These dimensions are each indispensable, and progress along one of the dimensions cannot be considered to compensate for the lack of progress, or even regressions, in other dimensions.

This corresponds to the major distinction between weak and strong sustainability in the seminal work of Herman Daly (1976, 2005). Simply put: while the conventional approach considers these dimensions as potential substitutes, where one can be replaced by another, in the strong sustainability approach, the viability of each needs first to be satisfied separately before reflecting on additional trade-offs between the dimensions. This contrast between the conventional weak sustainability and the strong sustainability approach is illustrated in Tables 6.1 and 6.2.

One year before the publication of the Stiglitz-Sen-Fitoussi report, an international team of 28 sustainability scholars released another important publication that brought the question of the baseline thresholds to international attention. These scientists identified and qualified a set of nine planetary boundaries within which humanity can continue to develop and thrive for generations to come (Rockström et al., 2009; for an update relying on the same approach, see Steffen et al., 2015). As stated by the authors, these nine boundaries do not aim at dictating how human societies should develop, but they can guide decision-making by defining a safe operating space for humanity as a precondition for sustainable development. Technically speaking, these nine boundaries define tipping points of human activity beyond which there is a risk of irreversible and abrupt environmental change within continental- to planetary-scale systems. To remain within such a safe operating space, human activities will need to limit the following changes in the Earth system process that are essential for human survival:

Table 6.1 The mainstream approach to sustainable development: maximizing the satisfaction of human needs of present and future generation, by improving one dimension (social, economic, environmental) or substituting one dimension for another

	Social dimensions	⇔	*Economic dimensions*	⇔	*Environmental dimensions*
Weak sustainability framework	Social factors contributing to satisfying human needs	Trade-off / substitution	Economic factors contributing to satisfying human needs	Trade-off / substitution	Environmental factors contributing to satisfying human needs

Source: By the authors, inspired by Daly (1976, 2005).

Table 6.2 Strong sustainability framework: sustaining the viability of each of the dimensions (social, economic, environmental, process), for present and future generations, above a set of minimum viable thresholds

	Socio-economic dimensions		**Economical dimensions**		**Process dimensions**
Minimum viable thresholds framework	Minimum conditions for enabling human well-being for all	AND	Minimal viable thresholds to stay within planetary boundaries	AND	Minimum guarantees for effective participation of disempowered
References from some key scholars	Stiglitz et al., 2010		Rockstrom et al., 2009		Scholsberg, 2009 (Environmental justice literature)
Components	Social connection Material well-being, etc.		Balance of the global Nitrogen cycle Sustainable freshwater use, etc.		Access to justice Empowerment of disenfranchised Capacity building, etc.

Source: By the authors, inspired by Daly (1976, 2005).

1 ocean acidification (through a dissolution of CO_2 in the oceans);
2 climate change (through an increase in the concentration of greenhouse gases in the atmosphere);
3 reduction in the stratospheric ozone (mainly caused by the release of gasses such as chlorofluorocarbons (CFCs) used as solvents for instance in dry cleaning and bromofluorocarbons used for its fire extinguishing properties);
4 land system change (soil degradation and soil loss);
5 loss of biological diversity;
6 decrease of global freshwater;
7 chemical pollution;
8 atmospheric aerosol (fine particles in the air);
9 chemical production of nitrogen (N) and phosphorus (P), flowing in excess into the natural nitrogen and phosphorus cycles.

This "planetary boundaries" approach defines what the authors call a "safe operating space for humanity": it is within these boundaries that just and sustainable societal choices should be made. However, the framework still lacks the crucial consideration of the *process* element of social choice. The environmental justice movement rightly emphasizes the importance of both taking stock of substantial progress (in terms of the dimensions of sustainable well-being and the planetary boundaries) and ensuring fairness and equity in the decision-making processes, as societies seek to strike a balance between the various dimensions of the multidimensional scoreboard referred to above. Indeed, insofar as the environmental justice movement focuses on the right to participate to environmental decision making in a fair and equitable matter and on struggles for recognition, it goes beyond the aggregative and distribute justice criteria already embodied in the sustainable well-being approach of the Stiglitz-Sen-Fitoussi report: the dashboard of well-being dimensions still falls short of telling us enough about the fairness or equity in the process involved when collectively determining the content of the major well-being dimensions, or about the freedom of citizens to invoke and utilize procedures that are equitable (Sen, 2009: 296).

By adding these two "operating space" constraints – the fairness of the decision-making process and the planetary thresholds – to the core well-being dimensions reviewed in the Stiglitz-Sen-Fitoussi report, one obtains a vision of a path for improving human well-being within a safe and just operating space. When integrated into such an "operating space", the burgeoning work by leading scholars and social actors over the last decade on alternative progress indicators and frameworks can provide an appropriate starting point to guide the collective reflection on the orientation of the social innovation and learning processes for transition (Figure 6.1).

Stimulating citizens-led social innovations: the 18th SDG

The Sustainable Development Goals include a Target, under SDG 17, to "encourage and promote effective public, public-private and civil society partnerships, building on the experience and resourcing strategies of partnerships" (Target 17.17). How can the transformative potential of such partnerships be maximized? Certain provisional conclusions stand out from empirical work done on transitions based on citizens-led social innovations. First, the *ad hoc* provision of support to grassroots innovations, or the establishment of forms of collaboration between private or public organizations and such innovations is not a substitute for strategic planning, understood as the definition of a long-term vision for change, allowing for adaptation to changing circumstances and a process of permanent learning. In other terms,

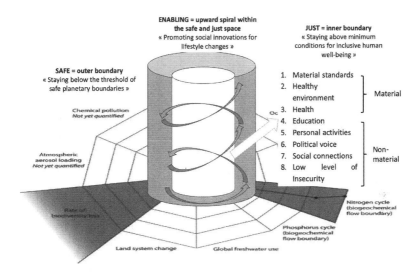

ENABLING = upward spiral within
the safe and just space
« Promoting social innovations for
lifestyle changes »

JUST = inner boundary
« Staying above minimum
conditions for inclusive human
well-being »

SAFE = outer boundary
« Staying below the threshold of
safe planetary boundaries »

Chemical pollution
Not yet quantified

Atmospheric
aerosol loading
Not yet quantified

Rate of
biodiversity loss

Land system change   Global freshwater use

Nitrogen cycle
(biogeochemical
flow boundary)

Phosphorus cycle
(biogeochemical
flow boundary)

Oc

1. Material standards
2. Healthy
   environment   ⎤
                           ⎥ Material
3. Health   ⎦
4. Education
5. Personal activities
6. Political voice   ⎤
7. Social connections   ⎥ Non-
8. Low   level   of   ⎦ material
   Insecurity

Figure 6.1 Framework for assessing: (1) the enabling of social innovations; (2) within a space of socially just and (3) environmentally sustainable human well-being. Figure by the authors.

pathway thinking is essential. Such pathway thinking is reducible neither to the small steps towards sustainability that could be taken, accommodating the various interests at stake, in a strictly pragmatist mode (in the common, non-philosophical meaning of the expression) nor to a grand vision that provides a blueprint for a desirable future. Rather, what is characteristic of pathway thinking is the combination of both: the vision gains credibility from the effort to identify the different steps that should be taken to achieve it, and the small steps in turn gain significance and relevance by being linked to the bold vision that gives them meaning.

Second, the institutional forms through which community-based initiatives can cooperate with private or public organizations vary widely, whether such forms of cooperation are bilateral or tripartite. Beyond the institutional variations, however, there lies a fundamental choice between forms of collaboration in which each of the actors maintains its own definition of its interests, and thus only seeks to forge an agreement that shall maximize its ability to achieve its (pre-defined) objectives, and forms of collaboration that, instead, being the result of a co-construction of joint objectives, lead each actor to redefine its interests. Forms of collaboration that can be truly transformative require a form of learning from actors that goes beyond a classic understanding of collaboration, in which each party contributes, in accordance with its interests and following a form of division of labor maximizing efficiency, to the achievement of objectives imposed from the outside (in particular, imposed by the profit-driven and competitive economy): they impose, beyond *collaboration* in the narrow sense of the expression, a form of *cooperation* which should be understood as involving a joint deliberation about the objectives, that should be set collectively by the actors (Laurent, 2018). Scholars working on the corporate community involvement thus distinguish various levels of partnerships between corporations and non-profit organizations seeking to respond to certain community needs, ranging from the philanthropic partnership (a "one-sided relationship" in which "the company donates and the nonprofit organization receives") to the transactional relationship (leading to a win-win solution, with the non-profit becoming a business partner), and from there to the integrative relationship, in which "the partners have a shared vision, and the missions of the organizations are coordinated with each other". The final phase is referred to as "transformational", in which:

> Partners work together to address socially relevant issues, paying considerable attention to the unique role that the cooperative partners have in this context. In this type of cooperation, the partners jointly identify a social issue that is relevant to both parties, in addition to determining the manner in which social innovation could contribute to a transformation in the community.
>
> (Roza et al., 2014: 17–18)

Third, where the collaboration results in the establishment of a joint project, the governance of such project may be more or less inclusive and thus allows more or less adequate for the project to be designed and implemented by taking into account expectations of the local actors. Tripartite forms of governance, in which communities, public authorities, and economic actors are all represented, are more robust: they are better equipped to face changing circumstances, as the various actors combine better their resources. They also create more trust between the participants (Ostrom, 2010; Bixler, 2014; Berardo and Lubell, 2016).

This SDG Target remains insufficient, however, in one important respect: it refers to the need to establish partnerships with civil society, but not to the creation of the conditions that could stimulate social innovations. Yet, for social innovations to emerge, a certain enabling environment may be required. Shaping this environment – what might be called an empowering architecture – may be a new role for the State, and one that is vital for accelerating the progress towards sustainable societies.

In the classic understanding of the functions of the State, the State is expected to intervene in cases of market failures (see, e.g., Sunstein, 1990): its role is to provide public goods that would be undersupplied by the market, including infrastructures but also a well-functioning public administration and health and education services affordable to all the population; to impose Pigovian taxes, thus ensuring an adequate internalization of negative externalities (i.e., the social, sanitary or environmental costs involved in the production process); to subsidize certain activities, in order to reward the societal benefits they provide (including the ecosystem services they render, or their contribution to social inclusion); to regulate market actors and to combat distortions of competition, thus ensuring that market power is not abused; and to adopt progressive taxation schemes, achieving the right balance between the need to reward risk and productive investment, on the one hand, and equality of opportunities on the other hand. It has also been argued, rightly, that beyond the "fixing" of market failures, the State has historically played an essential role in promoting innovation, in areas in which private investors may find too risky to venture, or where the returns on investment may be too low, or too distant in time. The role of the State, in this view, is not simply to step in where markets fail, but to create "new" markets, and to experiment, even if the risk may be to occasionally fail (Mazzucato, 2013).

While these functions are naturally vital, this inherited understanding of the relations between the State and the market remains too modest. It leaves intact the division of labour between the State and the market: whereas the State is to support the market and enable it to function correctly, the market actors are left free to define their own innovation pathways and to organize the production process in a way that maximizes the efficiency of production, and therefore their competitive position. However, left to itself, the process of innovation shall focus on the aspirations of the richest segments of the population, that have the ability to pay and thus to reward the innovators: it shall neglect the essential needs of the poor. Moreover, corporate-led technological innovations shall be poorly connected, if at all, to the lifestyle changes and to the social innovations that can steer societies towards a more sustainable form of development.

This is a major infirmity of the inherited understanding of the function of the State as "market facilitator", or as stepping in to remedy market failures. Such understanding neglects to consider the role of the

State as a facilitator, or a partner, of collective actions carried out by ordinary citizens or civil society actors. The State can create a favourable climate for the "pioneers" of transition. It can network initiatives that promote not only collective learning but also the co-construction by government and transition actors of regulatory and policy frameworks supporting these initiatives. It can also contribute to a transformation of social norms, accelerating the evolution towards pro-social and pro-environmental lifestyles, and thus creating a fertile ground for the emergence of social innovations that support such lifestyles. It can promote the emergence of collective action, including the management of certain goods and services governed as "commons", through the establishment of participatory modes of governance. An entirely new role for the State emerges: its role as an enabler of community and citizen-led social innovation.

References

Berardo, R. and Lubell, M. (2016). Understanding what shapes a polycentric governance system. *Public Administration Review, 76*(5): 738–751.
Bergius, M. and Buseth, T.J. (2019). Towards a green modernization development discourse: The new green revolution in Africa. *Journal of Political Ecology, 26*: 57–83.
Bixler, R.P. (2014). From community forest management to polycentric governance: Assessing evidence from the bottom up. *Society & Natural Resources, 27*(2): 155–169.
Brighouse, H. and Swift, A. (2006). Equality, priority and positional goods. *Ethics, 116*: 471–497.
Cassiers, I. (ed.) (2011). *Redéfinir la prospérité. Jalons pour un débat public.* Ed. de l'Aube: La Tour d'Aigues.
Castoriadis, C. (1975). *L'institution imaginaire de la société.* Paris: Seuil.
Chetty, R., Stepner, M., Abraham, S., Lin, S., Scuderi, B., Turner, N., Bergeron, A. and Cutler, D. (2016). The association between income and life expectancy in the United States, 2001–2014. *JAMA, 315*(16): 1750–1766. DOI: 10.1001/jama.2016.4226.
Corak, M. (2013). Income inequality, equality of opportunity, and intergenerational mobility. *Journal of Economic Perspectives, 27*(3): 79–102.
Daly, H.E. (1976). *Beyond Growth. The Economics of Sustainable Development.* New York: Beacon Press.
Daly, H.E. (1977). *Steady-State Economics.* Washington, DC: Island Press.
Daly, H.E. (2005). Economics in a full world. *Scientific American, 293*(3): 100–107.
Dolan, P., Peasgood, T. and White, M. (2008). Do we really know what makes us happy? A review of the economic literature on the factors associated with subjective well-being. *Journal of Economic Psychology, 29*: 94–122.

Easterlin, R. (1972). Does economic growth improve the human lot? Some empirical evidence. In: David, P. and Reder, M. (eds.). *Nations and Households in Economic Growth*: 89–126. Paolo Alto: Stanford University Press.

Easterlin, R. (1995). Will raising the incomes of all increase the happiness of all? *Journal of Economic Behaviour and Organization, 27*: 35–47.

Hickel, J. and Kallis, G. (2019). Is green growth possible? *New Political Economy*, DOI: 10.1080/13563467.2019.1598964.

Hirsch, F. (1976). *Social Limits to Growth*. Cambridge, MA: Harvard University Press.

Hirschman, A.O. (1982). *Shifting Involvements: Private Interest and Public Action*. Princeton, NJ and Oxford: Princeton University Press.

Hirschman, A.O. and Rothschild, M. (1973). The changing tolerance for income inequality in the course of economic development. *Quarterly Journal of Economics, 87*(4): 544–566.

Jackson, T. (2009). *Prosperity without Growth: Economics for a Finite Planet*. London: Earthscan.

Laurent, E. (2018). *L'impasse collaborative. Pour une véritable économie de la coopération*. Paris: Les Liens qui libèrent.

Laurent, E. and Le Cacheux, J. (2015). *Un nouveau monde économique. Mesurer le bien-être et la soutenabilité au XXIème siècle*. Paris: Odile Jacob.

Layard, R. (2005). *Happiness: Lessons from a New Science*. London: Penguin Books.

Loewenstein, G. (1987). Anticipation and the valuation of delayed consumption. *The Economic Journal, 97*(387): 666–684.

Mazzucato, M. (2013). *The Entrepreneurial State: Debunking Private vs Public Sector Myths*. London: Anthem Press.

Méda, D. (2013), *La mystique de la croissance: comment s'en libérer*. Paris: Flammarion.

Offe, C. (1987). The utopia of the zero-option: Modernity and modernization as normative political criteria. *Praxis International, 7*(1): 1–24.

Ostrom, E. (2010). Beyond markets and states: Polycentric governance of complex economic systems. *American Economic Review, 100*(3): 641–672.

Pelenc, J. and Ballet, J. (2015). Strong sustainability, critical natural capital and the capability approach. *Ecological Economics, 112*: 36–44.

Rockström, J., Steffen, W., Noone, K., Persson, Å., Chapin III, F.S., Lambin, E., Lenton, T.M., et al. (2009). Planetary boundaries: Exploring the safe operating space for humanity. *Ecology and Society, 14*(2): 32.

Roza, L., Stubbe, W. and Meijs, L. (2014). Why and how nonprofit organisations, companies and intermediaries can use Corporate Community Involvement to strengthen society. Research findings Rotterdam School of Management, Erasmus University Rotterdam.

Schlosberg, D. (2009). *Defining Environmental Justice: Theories, Movements, and Nature*. Oxford: Oxford University Press.

Scitovsky, T. (1976). *The Joyless Economy: The Psychology of Human Satisfaction*. Oxford and New York: Oxford University Press. (1992 revised edition.)

Sen, A. (2009). *The Idea of Justice*. Harvard: Harvard University Press.

Senik, C. (2008). Is man doomed to progress? Expectations, adaptation and well-being. *Journal of Economic Behaviour and Organization*, *68*(1): 140–152.

Senik, C. (2014). *L'économie du bonheur*. Coll. "La République des Idées". Paris: Seuil.

Steffen, W., Richardson, K., Rockström, J., Cornell, S.E., Fetzer, I., Bennett, M.E., Biggs, R., et al. (2015). Planetary boundaries: Guiding human development on a changing planet. *Science*, *347*(6223), DOI: 10.1126/science.1259855.

Stiglitz, J.E., Sen, A. and Fitoussi, J.-P. (2009). *Report by the Commission on the Measurement of Economic Performance and Social Progress*. Paris: Commission on the Measurement of Economic Performance and Social Progress.

Sunstein, C.R. (1990). *After the Rights Revolution: Reconceiving the Regulatory State*. Cambridge, MA: Harvard University Press.

Thiry, G. (2017). Ecological economics: Thinking of the post-growth era and its new sustainability indicators. In: Cassiers, I., Méda, D. and Maréchal, K. (eds.). *Post-Growth Economics and Society: Exploring the Paths of a Social and Ecological Transition*: 80–95. London: Routledge.

UN (2019). (Independent Group of Scientists appointed by the Secretary-General), Global Sustainable Development Report 2019. *The Future Is Now: Science for Achieving Sustainable Development*. New York: United Nations.

Weber, H. and Weber, M. (2020). When means of implementation meet ecological modernization theory: A critical frame for thinking about the sustainable development goals initiative. *World Development*, *136*: 105129.

7 The State as enabler of social innovations

Societal transformation based on citizens-led social innovations, on the one hand, a strong role of the State in organizing the transformation, on the other hand, should not be seen as competing views: they can and should be treated as complementary. The State may play an *enabling* role, facilitating citizens-led social innovations and ensuring their potential contribution to societal transformation is maximized. Four tools in particular can be used in this regard: the reduction of inequalities; urban planning and, more broadly, spatial organisation; encouraging experimentation by local collectivities; and changing the organizational culture of public administration.

Reducing inequality

To understand what this enabling role of the State may consist in, we should start by acknowledging the important links between the reduction of inequalities and the ecological transition. The link is obvious once we consider that the more equally the creation of wealth is spread across the population, the easiest it is to reconcile economic growth with poverty-reduction objectives: if the benefits of increased prosperity trickle down to the worse off in society, less growth will be required for the basic needs of all to be met. And since growing the economy cannot be done without increasing the use of resources and the production of waste, including greenhouse gas emissions responsible for climate changes (Jackson, 2017: chapter 5; Hickel and Kallis, 2019), it is imperative that, where the economy still must grow – where poverty reduction depends on the further creation of wealth –, it does so in ways that will maximize its positive impacts on lifting people out of poverty and that will minimize its ecological impacts. Moreover, the use of resources is more efficient in more equal societies. We have already noted that the allocation of resources through market

DOI: 10.4324/9781003223542-7

mechanisms serves to satisfy demand, as expressed by the purchasing power of the wealthiest parts of the population, rather than to respond to the needs of the poorest. This distorts our sense of priorities: in unequal societies, the "desires" of the most affluent may take precedence over the satisfaction of basic needs linked to housing, health, education, or access to green areas for the least affluent. Greater equality mitigates this distortion. Designing pro-poor policies and combating inequalities can therefore serve to mitigate the tension between ecological sustainability and poverty reduction, and ensure that whatever economic growth there is shall effectively improve the situation of the poor, rather than fuel consumption by the rich.

There is more to be said, however, on the links between equality and sustainability. Inequality makes people more materialistic and stimulates unsustainable modes of consumption. It inhibits civic and political participation, although participation is essential to ensure that large-scale transformations are sufficiently legitimate and supported across all society. Conversely, more equal societies encourage pro-social and pro-environmental behaviour: people in more equal societies express a greater concern for others and for the common good, which makes it easier for them to contribute to the achievement of certain collectively defined objectives. Equality is therefore the first, and perhaps most important, enabler of citizens-led social innovations.

Inequality and consumption

Inequality stimulates status competition and thus material consumption. We "want" material things, for the most part, not because of the comfort they provide alone, but for the message we send to those around us by owning or using them. This was a key insight of Veblen in his *Theory of the Leisure Class*: "the standard of expenditure which commonly guides our efforts", he wrote more than a century ago,

> is not the average, ordinary expenditure already achieved; it is an ideal of consumption that lies just beyond our reach, or to reach which requires some strain. The motive is emulation – the stimulus of an invidious comparison which prompts us to outdo those with whom we are in the habit of classing ourselves.
>
> (Veblen, 1899: 64)

Since "each class envies and emulates the class next above it in the social scale, while it rarely compares itself with those below or with those who are considerably in advance" (id.), unequal societies lead to a permanent race for status through consumption: social psychology has demonstrated that we attach more importance to our position in comparison to others against whom we rank ourselves than to our absolute levels of consumption alone (Solnick and Hemenway, 1998; Dolan et al., 2008). Conversely, if we achieve greater equality, or if we move towards a society in which social positioning can be signalled by means other than consumption, growth becomes less necessary (Wilkinson and Pickett, 2009a: 226).

The Stiglitz Commission on the Measurement of Economic Performance and Social Progress noted that the failure to value the reduction of inequality appropriately in our classic measures of progress could explain, in part, the gap between official statistics focusing on the aggregate level of performance of the economy and the subjective perception of well-being:

> When there are large changes in inequality (more generally a change in income distribution), gross domestic product (GDP) or any other aggregate computed per capita may not provide an accurate assessment of the situation in which most people find themselves. If inequality increases enough relative to the increase in average per capital GDP, most people can be worse off even though average income is increasing.
>
> (Stiglitz et al., 2009: 8)

But the problem lies deeper than that: even if the situation of a particular individual in fact improves *in absolute terms*, but remains stagnant (or, even worse, falls) *in relation to the other members of society*, that individual may experience a loss in well-being that the increased purchasing power, and thus the improvement in material conditions, may not compensate for. We already noted above, referring to the work of R. Easterlin and R. Layard, that in high-income countries, GDP growth had become unrelated to measures of subjective well-being, or what is commonly referred to as "happiness". One reason for this, as noted by Tim Jackson, is that unless it is combined with greater equality, income growth is a 'zero-sum game': a growth in average incomes that would leave people as wide apart from one another would hardly satisfy their desire to compare favourably to those around them, and the gains in life satisfaction would be, at best, minimal (Jackson, 2017: 57; Wilkinson and Pickett, 2018: 226).

The pursuit of greater equality would thus translate into an increase in well-being, which the pursuit of economic growth alone has become unable to provide. It would also mean putting a brake on the most unsustainable lifestyles, that only the richest segments of the population can afford. A study shows that in France, taking into account not only direct energy consumption (in electricity, gas, and fuel) but also the material goods consumed, the total energy consumption of the 20% wealthiest households is 2.5 times higher than the total energy consumption of the 20% poorest households (Global Chance, 2013). Similar conclusions already emerged from an earlier study, which estimated that the emissions of the lowest quintile of the French population were on average one-third of that of the highest quintile (Lenglart et al., 2010). In the Swedish city of Gothenburg, the comparison between the average emissions of a high-income family with two cars living in a detached house, those of a low-income family without a car living in a rented apartment, and those of the average Gothenburg resident, showed that the footprint of low-income households was just over half that of the high-income household (Figure 7.1).

In other terms, inequality fuels status competition through consumption. It widens the gap between classic measures of economic progress and life satisfaction. And it encourages unsustainable carbon-intensive

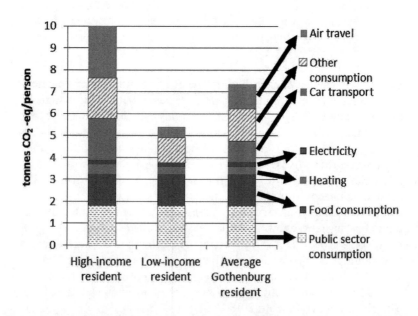

Figure 7.1 Emissions from the different typical households in Gothenburg in 2010, subdivided into different domains.

Source: Larsson and Bolin (2014).

lifestyles at the top, that become the norm that all other parts of the population aspire to. Instead, the more we channel macro-economic policies towards the reduction of inequalities, the more we can reconcile the duty of allowing each individual and family to live a decent life with the ecological imperatives of a finite planet. But there is more to this debate between equality and the ecological transition than its impact on lifestyles. More equal societies are also far better prepared to achieve the ecological transition than societies which tolerate high levels of inequality. There are three reasons for this.

Inequality and participation in civic and political life

No robust policies to tackle the growth of greenhouse gas emissions have a chance of succeeding unless they are perceived as legitimate by the population: as Richard Wilkinson and Kate Pickett note, "if policies to cut emissions are to gain public acceptance, they must be seen to be applied fairly" (Wilkinson and Pickett, 2009a: 221–222). Changes will be resisted unless the richest parts of the population, who are responsible for a disproportionate part of the greenhouse gases emitted, are made to contribute more than the others. In that sense, policies furthering greater equality should be seen as part of the package deal that will allow climate mitigation policies to gain widespread support across the population: "Greater equality can help us develop the public ethos and commitment to working together which we need if we are going to solve the problems which threaten us all" (Wilkinson and Pickett, 2009a: 233). Unfortunately, the current levels of inequality are such that they allow certain actors, who benefit most from the current patterns of distribution, to exercise a veto power on any significant redirection of the system, especially when they have most to lose from such a change: it is indeed these actors, whose lifestyles shall have to change, that can most easily capture political decision-making. Thus, whereas greater equality is a condition for change, it is also what makes it appear threatening to certain powerful actors, who often occupy dominant positions allowing them to block, or delay, the needed transformations.

This is in part because these actors act guided by their self-interest. It is also because information about the need for a shift, given the current rate of resource depletion that results from our lifestyles, is grasped less easily by those who intuitively perceive such messages about the unsustainability of our current patterns of growth as threatening not only their way of life but also their worldview. This is the phenomenon described in social psychology as the "white male effect" in the perception of environmental risk (Kahan et al., 2007). The expressive is of course slightly provocative; it is not however entirely without justification. As explained by Kahan et al. (2007: 467):

> individuals are disposed selectively to accept or dismiss risk claims in a manner that expresses their cultural values. It is natural for individuals to adopt a posture of extreme skepticism, in particular when charges of societal danger are leveled at activities integral to social roles constructed by their cultural commitments. The insensitivity to risk reflected in the white-male effect can thus be seen as a defensive response to a form of cultural identity threat that afflicts hierarchical and individualistic white males.

Privileged groups within society are less fearful of risk not only because they are, objectively, less at risk than others: they are also less fearful because they have more to lose than others from the lifestyle changes that are required for growth to be made compatible with the preservation of the natural resource base on which we depend. In contrast, equal societies are better equipped to transform themselves, since these groups will, by definition, have less power to oppose change.

Unequal societies are therefore less well equipped to achieve the transformation required because power in such societies tends to be monopolized by a narrow elite eager to preserve its dominant position, unwilling to accept challenges to its high-carbon lifestyle and to its meritocratic view of the world, and tempted to deny the reality of the risks entailed by environmental degradation. Moreover, the higher the level of inequality, the more participation in civic and political life by ordinary people, particularly among low-income groups, is discouraged (Alesina and La Ferrara, 2000; Uslaner and Brown, 2005). Members of such groups have fewer resources to spend on participation in civic life: they lack time, they face high opportunity costs, and they have a low level of trust in their ability to make a difference. The result is a form of retreat from civic and political life that soon creates a vicious cycle: as the cultural elites and high-income groups dominate the political scene, members of low-income groups are further unwilling to invest in a sphere which they feel is unresponsive to their needs and aspirations. In addition, the higher the level of inequality within society, the less its members see themselves as sharing common goals with others, which constitutes a further disincentive to civic participation (Rothstein and Uslaner, 2005).

Researchers have thus hypothesized that civic and political participation shall be lower among low-income groups due to a lack of resources, and that it shall be lower in more unequal societies, due to the fact that the "common good" is less clearly identifiable in more stratified societies. But which of these two mechanisms is the most powerful, since both generally go hand in hand? Based on a 2006 survey of 137,000 individuals in 24 European countries, Bram Lancee and Herman van de Werfhorst, both researchers at the University of Amsterdam, sought to measure the relationship between levels of inequality and civic participation for different income groups, taking into account also the fact that the resources available for participation may result from various forms of support provided by the Welfare State – such as subsidies for associations. Civic participation was measured on the basis of five criteria: participation in civic or neighbourhood associations, environmental groups, etc.; dedication of voluntary time to charitable causes; participation in recreational groups or associations such as sports clubs, etc.; involvement in political parties or associations or in trade unions; finally, participation in professional organizations. The survey confirms a close correlation between the level of inequality and the degree of civic participation (Figure 7.2).

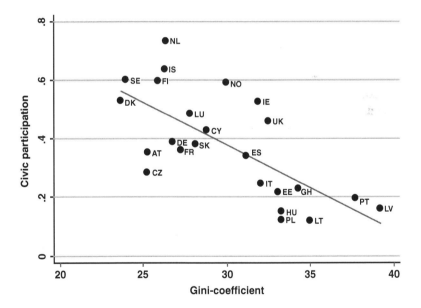

Figure 7.2 The relationship between civic participation and levels of inequality in 24 European countries.

Source: Lancee and van de Werfhorst (2011).

Note: The Mean Distance to the Median Income (MDMI) reflects the mean "distance" of a household income relative to the median household income in a respective country. It is mathematically very similar to the Gini coefficient, the most common measure of the level of inequality in a country.

In order to disentangle explanations for this correlation that emphasize the lack of resources people need to invest in various forms of civic participation (the so-called "neo-material" explanation, see Lynch et al., 2000), from explanations that emphasize instead the role of inequality as such, one would need of course to control these results against a number of variables, including age, work status, GDP per capita in the country concerned, degree of urbanization (from the least populated rural areas to the more densely populated urban areas), and the level of social expenditure per capita (in other terms, the weight of the Welfare State). Lancee and van de Werfhorst conclude from their careful attempt to separate these different explanations that the degree of inequality in a society is a key explanatory factor for differences in civic participation, even apart from the resources available to individuals. They conclude that "besides individual resources (income, education), more inequality at the top is associated with a lower likelihood to be active in a voluntary organization" (Lancee and van de Werfhorst, 2011: 29). More equal societies show higher participation rates, and "the depressing effect of above-median inequality on participation is invariant across income groups. Or, in other words, the association between income and civic participation is not dependent on the level of above-median income inequality" (id.); nor shall it be significantly influenced by the provision of social services that increase the availability of resources in particular for low-income groups. At the same time, "the positive effect of below-median equality on civic participation is stronger for low-income households than for high-income households": in other terms, it is primarily low-income groups whose degree of civic participation, including participation in political life, shall increase following a reduction in inequality levels (id.).

Inequality and other-regarding behaviour

In more equal societies, people are more willing to help others, and triggering pro-environmental behaviour is easier. In 2009, based on a comparison of the behaviour of affluent citizens across the different States of the United States, Alina Oxendine already highlighted that in more equal States, people were more prepared to help others (Oxendine, 2009). A few years later, Marii Paskov and Caroline Dewilde, two researchers of the University of Amsterdam, used data from the European Values Survey covering 26 European countries to assess the relationship between levels of inequality in society and solidarity, which they defined as "willingness to contribute to the welfare of other people". They concluded that, controlling for household income, GDP per capita, or the levels of social welfare expenditure in the country concerned (as a percentage of GDP), people living in more equal societies expressed greater willingness to help others than people living in more unequal societies (Paskov and Dewilde, 2012). Solidarity was measured based on the surveyed people's answer to the question: "Would you be prepared to actually do something to improve the conditions of: (a) people in your neighbourhood/community; (b) elderly in your country; (c) sick and disabled people in your country; (d) immigrants in your country?". The result linking levels of inequality within a particular society to lower levels of solidarity holds both for high-income households and for low-income households: it is thus not simply a mirror of the resources that the surveyed individuals are able to command. The results are summarized in the following graphs (Figure 7.3).

What appears true for pro-social behaviour appears true also for pro-environmental behaviour. Wilkinson and Pickett refer to studies that show a positive correlation between equality and the practice of recycling (Wilkinson and Pickett, 2009a: 232, referring to Planet Ark, 2004); and they note that, in more equal States, business leaders are more supportive of governments complying with multilateral environmental agreements (Wilkinson and Pickett, 2009b: 228–229). Together with Roberto de Vogli, they note the following relationship between income inequality and the importance business leaders attach to such compliance, on the basis of a survey of the World Economic Forum (World Economic Forum, 2002; Figure 7.4).

One reason why equality matters to resilience is also that social capital – the relations of trust, reciprocity, and exchange, forming the "glu" holding communities together, allowing for the evolution of common rules, and supported by networks, both formal and informal – functions as a sort of insurance policy in the face of risk and uncertainty: social capital matters for the sharing of knowledge, of financial risk, and of market information, and it also allows reciprocity-based forms of support to operate in times of crisis (Pretty and Ward, 2001; Adger, 2003). Indeed, informal networks and collective decision-making within communities can occasionally compensate for a dysfunctional state, as illustrated in coastal northern Vietnam by the building of sea dikes (Adger et al., 2001); or allow a community to maintain infrastructure such as roads and bridges, electricity lines, water supply, as for instance in the village of Santa Ana in Paraguay (Baldwin and King, 2017: 26).

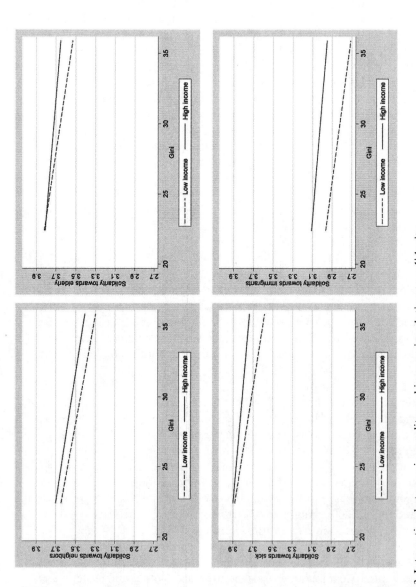

Figure 7.3 Interaction between inequality and income in relation to solidarity.
Source: Paskov and Dewilde (2012).

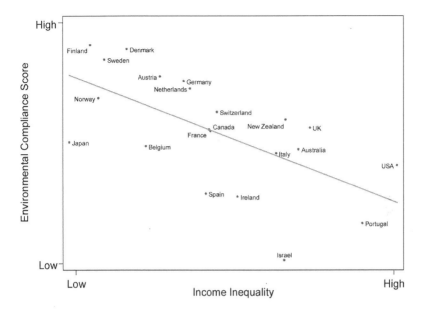

Figure 7.4 Relationship between environmental compliance score (importance business leaders attach to compliance with international
environmental agreements) and income inequality.
Source: Wilkinson et al. (2010).

Organizing space

How space is organized also has a major impact on the potential of
social innovation. Many regions have witnessed a significant urban
sprawl over the past decades, extending the distance between home
and other centres of activity – work of course, but also schools, shop-
ping facilities, and cultural or sports centres. This has a direct impact
on the ecological footprint of each individual: it requires the building
of considerable infrastructures to ensure sufficient connectivity – the
highways, the parking lots, and the gas stations – and it results in a
high dependence on the individual car. Such spatial extension is also
an obstacle to the growth of civic involvement and of involvement in
social innovations.

The strong relationship between urban planning and social innovations can be explained by a number of factors. First, commuting takes
time, and that time cannot be decided by community activity. Based
on self-reporting of Americans about their use of time, Robert Putnam
estimates that each additional ten minutes spent daily on commuting

diminishes involvement in community affairs by 10%: people spending an hour and a half in transport every day have basically no time left for attending meetings with neighbours, volunteering in local associations, or even keeping abreast of community affairs (Putnam, 2000: 213). Second, the geographical segregation that results from urban sprawl – with greener suburban areas essentially populated by the upper-middle class, and the working class concentrated either in polluted city centres or in the low-cost housing belts immediately surrounding the city centres –, means that there shall be fewer opportunities to build collective action across social and ethnic lines: bridging social capital, in particular, might be significantly eroded as a result (Putnam, 2000: 214). Third, once an individual's activities are spread across home, work, the children's school, and leisure, all located apart from one another, the incentives to invest in local community affairs shall be significantly diminished: one simply shall feel less part of the community within which one resides, if one works in another vicinity, or if the school of the children is located in yet another neighbourhood. Conversely, more social capital leads to increased participation in community affairs (Putnam, 1993).

There is a direct relationship between community attachment (Trentelman, 2009: 201), which arises from repeated interactions with other community members (Kasarda and Janowitz, 1974: 328), and pro-community behaviour, defined as "acts that are beneficial to the community at large as well as to other community residents" (Oishi et al., 2007: 831).

The organization of cities itself may or may not encourage informal contacts among neighbours. The more communal spaces are open, and the more cities' residents are provided opportunities to contribute to certain activities – including the management of such spaces, the setting up of events, or the design of long-term projects for the organization of the city –, the more barriers between communities will break down and the more social capital shall grow. Spatial organization has a key role to play in this regard: in the United States, the Progressive Era's emphasis in the early years of the 20th century on the development of playgrounds for children, museums, and public parks, was intended to stimulate the communitarian spirit, away from the individualistic ethos of the earlier era. Playgrounds, one enthusiastic advocate stated in 1912,

> bring about fine community spirit, awaken civic consciousness and co-operation, and make for whole-souled companionship instead of individualism and isolation. If we could see the playground idea

prevail... the gain to the nation through the ever increasing number of cheerful, contented, industrious, patriotic citizens will be far greater than if mined of fabulous wealth were uncovered or all the commerce of the world were brought under our flag.

(Putnam, 2000: 395, citing Scudder, 1912: 185–6)

The organization of urban space and the built environment have often been examined using the lens of social equity, to denounce the gaps between affluent and well-served neighbourhoods and areas of deprivation, with poorer living environments and reduced access to a range of public services and facilities for residents (Macintyre et al., 1993; Brook Lyndhurst, 2004). Spatial organization however can also be examined by asking whether it supports stronger social interactions, and thus encourages pro-community behaviours. (The EU Member States agreed on a definition of "sustainable communities", according to which such communities are

places where people want to live and work, now and in the future. They meet the diverse needs of existing and future residents, are sensitive to their environment, and contribute to a high quality of life. They are safe and inclusive, well planned, built and run, and offer equality of opportunity and good services for all.

(ODPM, 2006)

That standard definition in fact includes both social equity and social sustainability dimensions.)

Dempsey et al. (2009: 5–6; see also Bramley and Power, 2009) define sustainability of community as involving

social interaction between community members; the relative stability of the community, both in terms of overall maintenance of numbers/balance (net migration) and of the turnover of individual members; the existence of, and participation in, local collective institutions, formal and informal; levels of trust across the community, including issues of security from threats; and a positive sense of identification with, and pride in, the community.

Building on this definition as well as on a broader understanding of "social sustainability" as "the extent to which a neighbourhood supports individual and collective well-being" (a measure which is influenced both by the design of the physical environment and by the way residents relate to each other and function as a community (Baldwin and King, 2017: 9, referring to Woodcraft, 2012: 35), Cathy Baldwin and Robin King (2017) examined for the World Resources Institute how the organization of urban space may contribute to the sustainability of community thus defined, as well as to the resilience of communities following environmental shocks. What does it mean to move to "socially aware planning", informed by social or health impact assessments?

These questions were already asked many years ago by the proponents of the "New Urbanism" agenda, who explicitly aimed at challenging the growth of the suburbs by denouncing its impacts on the erosion of social capital (Duany and Plater-Zyberk, 1991, 1992; Katz, 1994). Instead, this school insisted, the environment should be built in order to create a "sense of community", since "communication networks are simply no substitute for real neighbourhood" (Talen, 1999: 1361). The principles of New Urbanism are well captured in Table 7.1.

Spanning 12 countries, the Baldwin-King study shed light on eight shared pro-community behavioural and psychological dimensions of a community that is both socially sustainable and resilient. Communities are better prepared to engage in large-scale and rapid transformations, this research showed, where individuals are strongly connected to their neighbourhood and the community – where they are proud of those connections and have a sense of belonging; where strong and frequent social interactions occur between neighbours; where people feel safe and secure, rather than fear the risks associated with change; where there is residential stability, in other terms, where the rate of transition from one place to another remains limited; where community members actively participate in community life, through civic action; where social cohesion is strong; where there exists a robust social solidarity, or community spirit; and where community members have a subjective sense of happiness and well-being, can exercise voice and influence, and are civically empowered. The comparison not only illustrates the important role of the State in spatial planning, and how this is one major tool to enable social innovations: it also provides further confirmation of the complementarity between higher levels of civic participation and the ability for societies to transform themselves.

Experimenting locally

France is generally perceived as a country which has a strong tendency towards the exercise of centralized power: though often described as "jacobine", by reference to the political faction that captured the French Revolution in 1789, this tendency in fact has much older roots

Table 7.1 The principles of New Urbanism

Aspect of the neighbourhood	Design principles	Social goal
Architecture and site design	Shrinkage of private space; houses close to street; small parking lots and short distances from the street; porches face street; individuality in house design	Encouraging residents to leave their houses and interact in the public sphere
Density and scale	Small-scale, well-defined neighbourhoods with clear boundaries and a clear centre; increased residential density	Resident interaction leading to a sense of community and neighbourliness
Streets	Viewed as public spaces; designed to encourage street life and increase in pedestrian activity; located in safe places	Pedestrian activity leading to feelings of safety, stronger community bonds, and a sense of place
Public space	Appropriate design and placement of public spaces such as parks and civic centres	Chance encounters between people, which strengthen community bonds; public spaces to be regarded as symbols of civic pride and sense of place, promoting community
Mixed land uses	A mixture of housing types; places of residence close to places to work, shop, and recreate	Encourages lingering and repetitive chance encounters; facilitates social interaction of people of different incomes, races, or ages; more walking and less driving; assists social integration, community bonds, and a sense of community

Source: Baldwin and King (2017: 30).

in the pre-revolutionary absolutist regime of the French monarchs, as powerfully demonstrated by Alexis de Tocqueville in the 1850s (de Tocqueville, 1955 (1856)).

Yet, it is France which, in 2003, led by example, in shaping the idea of the "local legislative experiment". A constitutional amendment, shortly followed by a framework legislation, allowed local entities to adopt certain public policies that are not in principle within their attributed competences, in order to develop certain "local experiments" for a defined period of time. The authorization given to local entities is strictly circumscribed: the enabling legislation should define the purpose of the experiment, the characteristics of the local collectivities allowed to experiment, the scope of the derogation from otherwise applicable legislative or regulatory provisions, as well as the maximum duration of the experiment, which cannot go beyond five years. If, following the experimentation period, the assessment is possible, a successful experiment can be made permanent and extended geographically to the territory: this is for instance how the *revenu de solidarité active*, a form of guaranteed minimum income, was introduced in 2007, initially in some regions only, before being generalized; and this is how a number of French municipalities, encouraged by the NGO All Together in Dignity (ATD) Fourth World, have been testing since 2015 the idea of "territories zero long-term unemployed" ("territoires zéro chômeurs de longue durée"), based on the idea that people in long-term unemployment were imposing higher direct and indirect costs on the collectivity than if subsidized employment opportunities were created for them, by the establishment of undertakings specifically dedicated to that purpose (called "entreprises à but d'emploi").

Such a "right to local experimentation", as it has been referred to in the French context, may be key to the emergence and to the flourishing of social innovations. Such innovations may never actually occur because the local actors have no blueprint to follow or no example to seek inspiration from: change, it sometimes seems, can only be immediately widespread (occurring across society), or infinitely postponed. Even more importantly, in areas such as food, energy, or mobility where citizens-led social innovations are the most relevant, such innovations can be obstructed because the competitive environment or the legal and regulatory frameworks are ill-adapted: temporary protections from such competition and temporary exemptions from these frameworks – precisely the philosophy underlying the "right to local experimentation" introduced in France in 2003 – may therefore be a condition for such innovations to develop and gradually, once they have been tested and proven successful, to become real alternatives.

Changing how public administration works

The Enabling State requires, finally, a new culture within public administration. This means much more than a rhetorical commitment to social innovation as a means to accompany and complement technological change. Governments at different levels have been increasingly interested in testing new solutions, and in designing governance mechanisms that will allow the permanent adaptation of solutions to changing circumstances: confronted with new problems, they seek to do things differently, constantly adapting the tools at their disposal. They increasingly refer to this as "social innovation", a label that has gained popularity since the turn of the century. However, "social innovation", if it means nothing else than that policy-makers are innovative in the approaches they experiment with, loses the dimension that we instead see as central: it does not empower communities. And there is a risk that, unless the administrative culture changes, it becomes a convenient catchword to designate any policy shifts, even when they are designed from above and bureaucratically imposed.

In contrast, we believe that the potential of "social innovation" as we explored it in this book, requires a changed administrative culture – one in which power is redistributed, and different sources of knowledge merged to produce new outcomes.

Of course, the administrative culture has not remained unchanged over the years. Quite to the contrary, various transformations did take place which accompanied the shift of the borders between the public and the private, linked initially to the growth of the Welfare State and nationalizations in the post-World War II era and, since the early 1980s, to privatization and the downsizing of the public sector. In order to align administrative culture with this latter shift, various alternatives have been proposed to the classic technocratic approach to public administration which characterized the rise of the bureaucratic State. New Public Management (NPM) is a form of public administration that emerged from the deregulation and the down-sizing of the public sector in the 1980s and 1990s, under both conservative and New Left governments. NPM presumed that by encouraging greater competition in public services (either by privatization or by disaggregating public administration into smaller sub-units and allowing them to compete against one another) and by allowing greater autonomy to public managers while measuring the results they achieve, efficiency gains could be achieved – in particular, the needs of the public would be better satisfied even with fewer resources at the disposal of the State.

More recently, and in part as a reaction to NPM, another approach saw the public not as "clients" whose demand is to be satisfied by introducing elements of competition in the delivery of public services, but as "stakeholders" whose views should be sought at various stages of policy design and implementation. Mark Moore, a professor at

Harvard's John F. Kennedy School of Government, introduced in 1995 the idea of "Public Value Management" (Moore, 1995), emphasizing the need to recognize the legitimacy of the views of a wide range of stakeholders in defining public value, as well as the need to permanently adapt to the delivery of public service to changing conditions: he thus proposed an approach that was "both post-bureaucratic and post-competitive" (O'Flynn, 2007: 353), premised on the idea that policy-makers ultimately were to be guided by a sense of public service ethos. This view rose in influence in the late1990s (Rhodes, 1997), and it characterized many of the reforms to European governance since the publication in July 2001 of the European Commission's White Paper dedicated to this topic (EC, 2001).

Some authors have accused Moore of giving too much weight to the judgment of public administrators as to what is in fact in the public interest – who, after all, would oversee the choices made by these "platonic guardians", as they were derisively called by some critics of Public Value Management (Rhodes and Wanna, 2009: 171), since there is no objective definition of what is in the public interest, except if we define it as the outcome of democratic politics –. Others, instead, have defended PVM as recognizing that elected politicians are ultimately accountable to the public, a question on which Moore himself was quite explicit:

> Politics remains the final arbiter of public value just as private consumption decisions remain the final arbiter of private value. Public managers can proceed only by finding a way to improve politics and to make it a firmer guide as to what is publicly valuable.
>
> (Moore, 1995: 38)

But what these two interpretations of PVM have in common is more significant than what separates them: whether unelected bureaucrats or elected politicians have the final say as to what is in the public interest, what predominates in both cases is a view of power as solid, or concentrated, and a view of policy-making as the implementation in specific contexts of certain predefined models. We now need something else: a view of power as liquid and distributed across society, and an understanding of "implementation" that takes seriously the permanent feedback loop between the formulation of policies and their application – a feedback in which the inventiveness and experiential knowledge of social actors are valued and built upon, rather than domesticated at worst and ignored at best.

Valuing "social innovation", in the more precise meaning of the expression retained here, would require an entirely distinct administrative culture. It would define the public as the "searchers", who "invent" solutions that can then be supported, built upon, and replicated by the public administration. The idea of "collaborative innovation" captures what is specific to this understanding: Nambisan sees it as a form of innovation in which government

> relies on harnessing the resources and the creativity of external networks and communities (including citizen networks as well as networks of nonprofits and private corporations) to amplify or enhance the innovation speed as well as the range and quality of innovation outcomes (or solutions).
>
> (Nambisan, 2008: 11, cited by Lévesque, 2013: 34)

This refers to shaping solutions to societal problems by involving people who are not treated merely as "beneficiaries" of public policies, nor as "clients" whose demand needs to be satisfied as in New Public Management (NPM) (Hood, 1991; Osborne and Gaebler, 1993), nor even as "stakeholders" to be consulted and involved in decision-making as in PVM, but as "actors", or "searchers", who make an active contribution to designing solutions, to implementing them in various contexts, and to assessing them. Just like we should be suspicious of the idea of markets simply registering the preferences expressed by consumers, as if those preferences were not shaped by the supply of goods and services and were untainted by the pressures exercised on tastes by the environment of the consumer society, we should be suspicious of the idea of politics simply registering the choices expressed by voters, as if those votes were not influenced by the citizens' perception of the existing range of institutional alternatives: social innovation, to expand, requires space, and a far less rigid division of labour between civil society, markets, and politics.

This is also the vision developed by the growing number of authors working on the "commons". There exists of course a narrowly economicist view of the "commons", which uses this expression to describe a certain category of goods or services that, because of certain characteristics (in particular, because they would be undersupplied by the market and mismanaged by the centralizing power of the State), are best governed by the users themselves; this is the perspective adopted by Elinor Ostrom who refers to "common pool resources" to describe such goods or services, and proposes that such resources should be managed by local communities, who set their own rules, enforced by the members (Ostrom, 1990). But the richer and more promising reference to the "commons" appears in the description of citizens-led initiatives that deliberately opt to move away from the State-market condominium described above and to create instead their own solutions based on values of solidarity and democratic self-governance. "Commoning", in that sense – the establishment and managing of the "commons" –, is about co-constructing solutions that follow neither the bureaucratic logic of public administration nor the profit-driven logic of markets. This requires what David Bollier and Silke Helfrich, who are among the most interesting exponents of the idea, call "peer governance", a means of setting rules and enforcing them, and of dealing with conflicts, in which "individuals see each other as peers with the equal potential to participate in a collective process, not as adversaries competing to seize control of a central apparatus of power" (Bollier and Helfrich, 2019: 85). Peer governance, they insist, is "distinct from governing *for* the people and from governing *with* the people [as in participatory modes of governance]. It is governing *through* the people" (Bollier and Helfrich, 2019: 85). Classic modes of State administration, they explain, are incompatible with the spirit of the "commons" thus understood:

> To be effective and trusted, state power cannot just impose bureaucratic master plans; it must learn how to foster relationships among real people who have their own creative agency. This requires that we get away from the idea of human beings as units of need to which 'service providers' must minister [...]. Focused on administering services, state agencies and service professionals tend to dismiss people's own creative talents, desire to contribute, and capacities for commoning. [They] neither recognize people's actual human agency nor strengthen that power. For their part, most people have internalized this image of themselves as passive consumers of professional and government services, and fail to regard themselves as potential participants in Peer Governance or the state polity.
>
> (Bollier and Helfrich, 2019: 291)

Putting social innovation at the heart of public policy-making substitutes co-design for simple feedback as in NPM, or for consultation as in multi-stakeholders approaches. Ordinary people, the social actors, are neither "governed", nor "clients" whose needs must be catered to, nor even "participants" invited to feed into a policy-making process in which enlightened administrators or politicians have the final work: they are "agents", setting their own rules and governance mechanisms. And what is expected from the State apparatus is not simply to "respect" such self-governance, in the minimal sense of not imposing obstacles, but to "enable", by identifying the remaining obstacles and removing them one by one. The following typology emerges (partly inspired by Lévesque, 2013: 33; Table 7.2).

* * *

Table 7.2 Various approaches to public administration and various understandings of the role of innovation

	Traditional public administration	*New public management (Public service users as consumers approach)*	*Public value management (Stakeholders approach)*	*Social innovations approach*
State	Interventionist, provider of public services and of market-correcting regulation	Limited (privatization and deregulation)	Open to dialogue with citizens	Facilitator of social experimentation, favouring the emergence of local solutions
Public	Beneficiaries of services and addressees of regulation	Clients expressing a demand through mechanisms mimicking the market	Citizens involved through participation/ consultation	Actors/ searchers, empowered to co-design new solutions
Public interest	Defined (vertically) through traditional electoral processes and principal-agent relationship between elected governments and public administration	Defined as the most efficient use of public resources, through cost-benefit analysis and by favouring choice of the public as a means to reveal their preferences	Defined (horizontally) through participatory means	Emerges bottom-up through local innovations that can be replicated and scaled up

(Continued)

	Traditional public administration	New public management (Public service users as consumers approach)	Public value management (Stakeholders approach)	Social innovations approach
Innovation	Technocrats in public administration come up with new ideas	The public rewards new solutions that satisfy its wants by "voting with their feet"	New ideas emerging from the top are "tested" by consulting with people, in focus groups or participatory fora	New ideas emerge "from below", at the initiative of citizens themselves or local-level governance units

This has been a strange journey. We started with the challenge set by Elinor Ostrom: how, she asked in 2009, can we design institutions that "bring out the best in humans"? We made clear our dissatisfaction with the mainstream responses to the challenge of establishing sustainable and resilient societies, which put all their hopes either in governments or in the "greening" of the economy – combining technological breakthroughs and critical consumerism, together with facilitating and encouraging corporate citizenship. These responses are not only insufficient by themselves. They also are deeply demobilizing: if governments and companies are moving in the right direction, gradually creating the right set of incentives and investing in the right lines of research to reduce our ecological footprint, why should the rest of us care? Why should ordinary women and men be concerned about their own role in the transition?

In contrast, we argued that citizens-led social innovations should be seen as a major instrument of societal transformation. But they are also an instrument whose potential remains largely untapped. Can more be done? In a way, this is a paradoxical question: if social innovations designed by ordinary people at the local level are key, then should this not, by definition, be left to "normal", spontaneous processes? As the old African proverb states, you don't grow a tree by pulling on its branches: you don't create innovation, nor do you stimulate initiatives by people, any more than you can predict what innovation will consist in or how people will be motivated to act. The more we delved into this question, however, the more we came to the conclusion that these were false oppositions. Innovation can be stimulated although we cannot know, by definition, how it will occur, and in which ways it will surprise us. And communities can be encouraged to act, although it would be counter-productive to force them into action. You don't grow a tree by pulling on its branches. But you can nurture the soil in which it takes root, and help it with some water during the dry season.

References

Adger, W.N. (2003). Social capital, collective action, and adaptation to climate change. *Economic Geography*, *79*(4): 387–404.

Adger, W.N., Kelly, P.M. and Ninh, N.H. (eds.) (2001). *Living with Environmental Change: Social Resilience, Adaptation and Vulnerability in Vietnam.* London: Routledge.

Alesina, A. and La Ferrara, E. (2000). Participation in heterogeneous communities. *The Quarterly Journal of Economics*, *115*: 847–858.

Baldwin, C. and King, R. (2017). *What about the People? The Socially Sustainable, Resilient Community and Urban Development.* Report. Oxford: Oxford Brookes University.

Bollier, D. and Helfrich, S. (2019). *Free, Fair and Alive. The Insurgent Power of the Commons.* British Columbia: New Society Publ.

Bramley, G. and Power, S. (2009). Urban form and social sustainability: The role of density and housing type. *Environment and Planning B: Planning and Design*, *36*: 30–48.

Brook Lyndhurst. (2004). *Research Report 11: Environmental Exclusion Review.* London: Office of the Deputy Prime Minister.

Dempsey, N., Bramley, G., Power, S. and Brown, C. (2009). The social dimension of sustainable development: Defining urban social sustainability. *Sustainable Development*, *19*: 289–300.

de Tocqueville, A. (1955). *The Old Regime and the French Revolution.* New York: Anchor Books (original publication in French: *L'Ancien Régime et la Révolution* (1856)).

Dolan, P., Peasgood, T. and White, M. (2008). Do we really know what makes us happy? A review of the economic literature on the factors associated with subjective well-being. *Journal of Economic Psychology*, *29*: 94–122.

Duany, A. and Plater-Zyberk, E. (1991). *Towns and Town-Making Principles.* New York: Rizzoli.

Duany, A. and Plater-Zyberk, E. (1992). The second coming of the American small town. *Wilson Quarterly*, *16*: 3–51.

EC (2001). *European Governance.* European Commission White Paper. COM (2001) 428 final, of 25.7.2001.

Global Chance. (2013). Des questions qui fâchent: Contribution au débat national sur la transition énergétique. *Les Cahiers de Global Chance*, *33*: 1–116.

Hickel, J. and Kallis, G. (2019). Is green growth possible? *New Political Economy*, DOI: 10.1080/13563467.2019.1598964.

Hood, C. (1991). A public management for all seasons? *Public Administration,* 69(1): 3–19.

Jackson, T. (2017). *Prosperity without Growth. Foundations for the Economy of Tomorrow.* London: Routledge.

Kahan, D.M., Braman, D., Gastil, J., Slovic, P. and Mertz, C.K. (2007). Culture and identity-protective cognition: Explaining the white-male effect in risk perception. *Journal of Empirical Legal Studies,* 4(3): 465–505.

Kasarda, J.D. and Janowitz, M. (1974). Community attachment in mass society. *American Sociological Review, 39:* 328–339.

Katz, P. (1994). *The New Urbanism: Toward an Architecture of Community.* New York: McGraw Hill.

Lancee, B. and van de Werfhorst, H. (2011). *Income Inequality and Participation: A Comparison of 24 European Countries.* (GINI discussion paper; No. 6). Amsterdam: AIAS.

Larsson, J. and Bolin, L. (2014). *Low-Carbon Gothenburg 2.0. Technological Potentials and Lifestyle Changes.* Mistra Urban Futures. Retrieved online: https:// www.mistraurbanfutures.org/en/publication/low-carbon-gothenburg-20-technological-potentials-and-lifestyle-changes

Lenglart, F., Lesieur, C. and Pasquier, J.-L. (2010). Les émissions de CO_2 du circuit économique en France. *Insee Références, Édition 2010.*

Lévesque, B. (2013). Social innovation in governance and public management systems: Towards a new paradigm? In: Moulaert, F., MacCallum, D., Mehmood, A. and Hamdouch, A. (eds.). *The International Handbook on Social Innovation. Collective Action, Social Learning and Transdisciplinary Research:* 25–39. Cheltenham, UK and Northampton, MA: Edward Elgar.

Lynch, J.W., Smith, G.D., Kaplan, G.A. and House, J.S. (2000). Income inequality and mortality: Importance to health of individual income, psychosocial environment, or material conditions. *BMJ, 320:* 1200–1204.

Macintyre, S., MacIver, S. and Sooman, A. (1993). Area, class and health: Should we be focusing on places or people? *Journal of Social Policy, 22:* 213–234.

Moore, M. (1995). *Creating Public Value: Strategic Management in Government.* Cambridge, MA: Harvard University Press.

Nambisan, S. (2008). *Transforming Government through Collaborative Innovation.* IBM Center for the Business of Government. Retreived online: https://www.businessofgovernment.org/report/transforming-government-through-collaborative-innovation

ODPM (Office of the Deputy Prime Minister). (2006). *UK Presidency: EU Ministerial Informal on Sustainable Communities Policy Papers.* London: ODPM.

O'Flynn, J. (2007). From new public management to public value: Paradigmatic change and managerial implications. *The Australian Journal of Public Administration,* 66(3): 353–366.

Oishi, S., Sherman, G.D., Rothman, A.J., Snyder, M., Su, J., Zehm, K., Hertel, A.W. and Hope Gonzales, M. (2007). The socioecological model of procommunity action: The benefits of residential stability. *Journal of Personality and Social Psychology,* 95(3): 831–844.

Osborne, D. and Gaebler, T. (1993). *Reinventing Government: How the Entrepreneurial Spirit is Transforming the Public Sector.* New York: Penguin.

Ostrom, E. (1990). *Governing the Commons. The Evolution of Institutions for Collective Action.* Cambridge, MA: Cambridge University Press.

Oxendine, A.R. (2009). Inequality and Indifference: America's Wealthy and Cross-Cutting Civic Engagement. In 67th Annual Meeting of the Midwest Political Science Association, The Palmer House Hilton, April 2nd.

Paskov, M. and Dewilde, C.L. (2012). *Income Inequality and Solidarity in Europe.* (GINI Discussion Paper; No. 33). Amsterdam: AIAS (later published Research in *Social Stratification and Mobility, 30*(4): 415–432).

Planet Ark. (2004). *The Recycling Olympic Report.* Sydney: Planet Ark Environmental Foundation.

Pretty, J. and Ward, H. (2001). Social capital and the environment. *World Development, 29*: 209–227.

Putnam, R.D. (1993). *Making Democracy Work: Civic Traditions in Modern Italy.* Princeton, NJ: Princeton University Press.

Putnam, R.D. (2000). *Bowling Alone: The Collapse and Revival of American Community.* New York: Simon Schuster.

Rhodes, R.A.W. (1997). *Understanding Governance. Policy Networks, Governance, Reflexivity and Accountability.* Maidenhead: Open University Press.

Rhodes, R.A.W. and Wanna, J. (2009). Bringing the politics back in: Public value in Westminster parliamentary government. *Public Administration, 87*(2): 161–183.

Rothstein, B. and Uslaner, E.M. (2005). All for all: Equality, corruption, and social trust. *World Politics, 58*: 41–72.

Scudder, M.T. (1912). Rural recreation: A socializing factor. *Country Life, 40*: 175–190.

Solnick, S.J. and Hemenway, D. (1998). Is more always better? A survey on positional concerns. *Journal of Economic Behavior & Organization, 37*: 373–383.

Stiglitz, J.E., Sen, A. and Fitoussi, J.-P. (2009). *Report by the Commission on the Measurement of Economic Performance and Social Progress.* Paris: Commission on the Measurement of Economic Performance and Social Progress.

Talen, E. (1999). Sense of community and neighbourhood form: An assessment of the social doctrine of New Urbanism. *Urban Studies, 36*(8): 1361–1379.

Trentelman, C.K. (2009). Place attachment and community attachment: A primer grounded in the lived experience of a community sociologist. *Society and Natural Resources, 22*(3): 191–210.

Uslaner, E.M. and Brown, M. (2005). Inequality, trust, and civic engagement. *American Politics Research, 33*: 868–894.

Veblen, T. (1899). *The Theory of the Leisure Class. An Economic Study of Institutions.* New York: Macmillan. (1994 edition by Dover Publ. New York).

Wilkinson, R. and Pickett, K. (2009a). *The Spirit Level. Why Greater Equality Makes Societies Stronger.* London: Allen Lane.

Wilkinson, R. and Pickett, K. (2009b). *Equality and Sustainability*. London: London Sustainable Development Commission.

Wilkinson, R. and Pickett, K. (2018). *The Inner Level. How More Equal Societies Reduce Stress, Restore Sanity and Improve Everyone's Well-being.* London: Allen Lane.

Wilkinson, R., Pickett, K. and de Vogli, R. (2010). Equality, sustainability, and quality of life. *British Medical Journal, 341*: 1138–1140.

Woodcraft, S. (2012). Social sustainability and new communities: Moving from concept to practice in the UK. *Procedia – Social and Behavioural Sciences, 68*: 29–42.

World Economic Forum. (2002). *The Global Competitiveness Report, 2001–2002*. Oxford: Oxford University Press.

Index